YORUBA FROM CUBA

ACKNOWLEDGEMENTS

This translation is dedicated to my dear mother
Doña María Carboneres Masiá

My thanks to Doña Natalia Roig Sanz who taught me to see beyond colour or creed. I would also like to thank all my friends and colleagues who helped me with their advice and encouragement. I am particularly grateful to Dr. Susan Bassnett for her enlightened guidance and assistance, and to Professor Alistair Hennessy for his introduction, notes and recommended reading.

Our thanks and gratitude to Nicolás Guillén's heirs for granting copyright permission and to Olga Lidia Triana of the Agencia Literaria Latinoamerica for facilitating the contact.

NICOLÁS GUILLÉN

YORUBA FROM CUBA

SELECTED POEMS
POESÍAS ESCOGIDAS

TRANSLATED BY
SALVADOR ORTIZ-CARBONERES

P E E P A L   T R E E

First published in Great Britain in 2005, reprinted 2010
Peepal Tree Press Ltd
17 King's Avenue
Leeds LS6 1QS
UK

ISBN 9781900715973

Supported by
ARTS COUNCIL
ENGLAND

INDICE

CONTENTS

7

TRANSLATING NICOLÁS GUILLÉN

Salvador Ortiz-Carboneres

Before thinking about translating Nicolás Guillén I had already made use of his poetry in the course of my language teaching. What attracted me to him in the first place was not only the uniqueness of his language, which I can compare only to that of Federico García Lorca, but also his commitment to the defence of noble causes, especially his concern for the plight of Black Americans.

Once I had decided to translate him extensively I had to make an in-depth study of his background, which took me back to his roots in Africa, and the effects of racial prejudice observed both in the Caribbean and the USA. I concentrated especially on this racial theme not only because I deeply believe in his message, but also in my opinion, this theme inspired the best poetry.

I would like to impress on the reader just how difficult the task of the translator is. The poems chosen here show evidence of the way Guillén uses incantatory rhythms in his poetry, and appeals to ancestral African patterns of language to provide the lyrical structure of his poetry. He uses the untranslatable term 'son' for this strong Cuban dance rhythm that pervades his whole work.

Translation, like the original process of creation, is a voyage of discovery. In translating Guillén, the keynote is expression – the expression of people through their everyday spoken language, through dance rhythms, and through the strong community spirit they weave. Guillén crystallizes all these elements in his work, and the translator is made acutely aware of their importance.

To me, as I am sure Guillén would agree, the greatest poetry in the world has its roots in the people (*el pueblo*), and the reader's understanding of it is like a voyage of return to the people. The line:

I am Yoruba from Cuba

points to the new spirit of integration following the impact of the 'negrismo' movement. Through the popular culture of music and dance, the dominant European culture in Cuba began to draw on the culture of Afro-Cubans, a group discovering a new pride an confidence. For a literary precursor of the strength found in African rhythm we have only to go back to Shakespeare and look at Caliban's speech from the end of Act 2 of *The Tempest*:

No more dams I'll make for fish;
  Nor fetch in firing
  At requiring,
Nor scrape trencher, nor wash dish:
'Ban, 'Ban Ca–Caliban,
Has a new master Get a new man.

The greatest difference is that in Guillén's poetry there are no masters and slaves – the black culture has become fused with the white – and there is a new pride in the black, from which the white also draws strength.

The translator must always show humility in the face of the text, especially when translating into a language which is not his or her mother tongue, and be ready to consult others in the search for alternative phrases. I always try and aim for three things: clarity, adequacy of expression, and unity. I start from the word, then move out from the word into the syntax, style, context and rhythm, and return finally to the resonance of the single word. This circular process of outward movement and return itself guarantees unity, and the correspondence of parts to the whole. Guillén has demonstrated in his poetry how important Afro-Caribbean roots are to the revitalisation of the Castilian language, a language he felt had lost touch with elemental forces still to be found in the popular African culture of Cuba. In translating him I felt that I too was on a voyage of discovery, or rather rediscovery, of my own language.

INTRODUCTION

Alistair Hennessy

When Nicolás Guillén died in July 1989 the Spanish-speaking world lost one of its great twentieth century poets. But he is not only a poet for the Hispanic world but for all those who are concerned with the themes of his poetry: racism, justice, vitality, creativity. His works, at least his poetry, have been translated into many languages and there are a number of versions in English, but this volume is only the second selection to be published in this country.

As Salvador Ortiz-Carboneres explains, his poems have been widely used in teaching Spanish at Warwick University, partly because he is direct and speaks to many of the issues which students study in their other work, but also because his innate rhythmic quality and simplicity make his poetry accessible to all. This simplicity, however, is deceptive – the eight poems of his first collection caused him immense trouble, as he explained to a querulous critic who complained of their lack of depth. There is now a burgeoning critical literature which is unearthing the deeper springs of his inspiration, but this introduction is not concerned with assessing his work in literary terms but rather to put it into a historical and social context, because without background readers may miss some of the deep resonances which have made him a giant among the immortals.

Nicolás Guillén was born in 1902, the year in which Cuba became an independent republic after nearly thirty years of incessant warfare against the Spaniards. Although the Cubans had borne the brunt of a savage guerrilla war involving civilians, which foreshadowed the total wars of the twentieth century it was United States' intervention in 1898, with their superior naval power, which finally defeated the Spaniards.

The price for their intervention was a humiliating peace treaty at which the Cubans were not even represented. The subsequent restriction of Cuban sovereignty by the Platt Amendment to the Cuban Constitution permitted the United States to intervene whenever they considered that their interests were threatened. This brooding presence was to dominate Guillén's imagination as it did for many other Cubans, especially those who were mulattos like Guillén.

The comment of W.E. Du Bois, America's leading Black intellectual, that colour would be the major issue of the twentieth century found early confirmation in Cuba. It is too often forgotten how the 1898 war coincided with the failure of Reconstruction in the American South, exemplified by the fact that the 1890s was the worst decade for lynchings, averaging over one hundred and eighty a year. When American troops contacted the Cuban Liberating Army, many of whom were mulattos and supposedly allies, American officers felt that they had been fighting the wrong enemy. Cubans were rebuffed and humiliated; Blacks became the butt of savage cartoons in the American press much as they had been in the Spanish press during the war. Some of these attitudes were shared by white Americanized Cuban exiles on their return to the island.

It was soon clear that Blacks were to have no place in the new Cuba. Instead of the bright vision of José Martí with its racial harmony, social justice, political democracy and liberation from dependence on external economic forces, the new nation was riddled with corruption, political inequality and social injustice. Blacks who had served in the army were often marginalized, acquiring neither land, education, nor a share in the political spoils which oiled the wheels of Cuban politics.

Overt racialism grew as new waves of Spanish immigrants flooded in as part of a whitening policy. Black immigration was forbidden by decree until labour was imported from Haiti and the British West Indies to meet the demands of expanding sugar plantations, now mostly under American ownership. Disillusion led to the formation of the PIC (Independent Party of Colour) but in order to stem its growth a law was passed in 1910 forbidding political parties to be based on colour. Ironically, it was named after Morúa Delgado, one of the few coloured intellectuals, who was President of the Senate. Further frustration erupted in the so-called Race War of 1912 in which as many as 3000 Blacks may have been killed. Faced by such discrimination Blacks withdrew into their own subculture based on secret societies. It was only with the emergence of an awareness of Cuba's African heritage as a key component of national identity in the 1920s that Blacks began to be more assertive with Guillén as their most distinctive voice.

Guillén was born into a modest middle class family in the cattle province of Camagüey in central Cuba, that 'idyllic countryside of shepherds and sombreros'. His parents were both mulattos and so, like many other Cubans, he was of mixed Hispanic-African ancestry. In contrast to the English-speaking Caribbean, Cuba was a settlement as well as a plantation colony, so that the presence of a large Spanish population, predominantly males, meant that miscegenation proceeded at a much faster pace than in other European colonies, and like so many with an unrecorded past he wondered about his African forbears:

Seré Yelofe?	Will I be Yelofe?
Nicolás Yelofe, acaso	Nicolás Yelofe, perhaps?
O Nicolás Bakongo?	Or Nicolás Bakongo?
Tal Vez Guillén Bakongo?	Perhaps Guillén Bakongo?
O Kumba?	Or Kumba?
Tal vez Guillén Kumba?	Perhaps Guillén Kumba?
O Kongue?	Or Kongue?
Pudiera ser Guillén Kongue?	Could I be Guillén Kongue?
Oh, quién lo sabe?	Oh, who knows?
Qué enigma entre las aguas?	What enigma lies among the waves?

His father was a journalist and a politician, a senator who in 1917 was shot in one of the many turbulent political conflicts of the time. After a brief spell at Havana University studying law, Nicolás returned to Camagüey to take up journalism. However, it was not until the late 1920s that his poetry reflected the anti-imperialism and Black consciousness which made him a new and original voice. Although race and slavery had preoccupied a number of Cuban writers in the mid-nineteenth century, most of these had been white. One important exception was Juan Francisco Manzano, a liberated slave whose remarkable autobiography had first been published in

English by the abolitionist Richard Madden in 1840 for the anti-slavery convention in London. The fact that it was not translated into Spanish until 1937 reflected the government's fear of slave risings. It was not until the 1880s, after the abolition of slavery, that reforms permitted the publication of Black newspapers, but the few Black journalists – one of whom, Morúa Delgado, was a considerable novelist – were still subject to capricious censorship and it was not until the 1920s that the political and cultural climate changed in the aftermath of the First World War.

The 1920s were to be a turning point in Cuba as in Latin America generally. Economic and social unrest accompanied the collapse of the World War sugar boom, providing new openings for the penetration of American capital. At the same time, gangsters driven out by Prohibition in the United States gave Havana its reputation as the red-light capital of the Caribbean. The crisis, economic, social and moral of the early twenties stimulated a new and strident anti-American nationalism fuelled by the examples of the Russian and Mexican Revolutions and the Latin American University Reform movement.

Already, a white ethnologist, Fernando Ortiz, through his researches into black culture, had begun to provide the basis for the elaboration of a distinctive nationalist ideology of *cubanía* which incorporated the African heritage. This was more inclusive than the concept of *cubanidad*, formulated in the 1830s, which conceived the nation to be white, exclusivist and Hispanic. An expression of this new African interest were the poems of the Puerto Rican Luis Palés Matos and the emerging negrista movement dating from 1925. Palés Matos and his Cuban counterparts, Ramón Guirao and José Tallet, were white, attracted like many Europeans to the novelties of the 'other' and the energy and exoticism of Africa, as expressed in music, dance and sculpture. In 1929, however, a poem appeared in the Havana press which marked the emergence of an authentic black voice – the first in Cuba since the brief flowering of black writers in the 1880s. Nicolás Guillén's poem 'Kid Chocolate' celebrated the fame of a Black Cuban boxer who had become a national hero through winning 109 out of 122 fights in America. It was later to be renamed as 'Small Ode to the Cuban Boxer' when it was republished in *Sóngoro Cosongo* (1931).

Ya ahora que Europa se desnuda
para tostar su carne al sol
y busca en Harlem y en La Habana
Jazz y son....

And now that Europe strips off
to bask in the sun
and searches in Harlem and Havana
for Jazz and *son*

This stanza catches the paradox of whites despising colour and yet wanting to acquire a tan, as well as pride in Black defeating white. Afro-Cubanism was part of that general black *prise de conscience* which found expression throughout the Americas in such diverse forms as Afro-Brazilianism and the Harlem Renaissance. It was through the latter that the Caribbean was linked to American Blacks through such figures as the Jamaicans Marcus Garvey and Claude McKay with their following in the burgeoning West Indian immigrant population in Harlem. But the major link between Black American writers and Cuba was Langston Hughes. Hughes met Guillén on his second visit to Havana early in 1930. At 28, the same age as Guillén, Hughes had already acquired a reputation as a promising Black poet. He was also familiar with Spanish and had visited Africa as a seaman. Through Fernández de Castro, a white editor who had been the first person to translate Hughes into Spanish, the two poets met. Hughes provided the final spur to Guillén to base his poetry on the dance rhythms of the *son,* a popular Afro-Cuban dance, and in doing so to catch the spirit and speech of Havana's poor Blacks, much as the blues did for their counterparts in the States. The eight poems *Motivos de Son* which appeared within a month of Hughes's visit created a scandal, partly because they were not published in an obscure 'little magazine' but in the Sunday supplement devoted to Black affairs in Havana's most conservative paper, the *Diario de la Marina,* then the equivalent *Times* of Cuba. His editor, Gustavo Urrutia, described

15

them as 'the best kind of negro poetry that we ever had: indeed we had no negro poems at all.' Among those outraged at choosing the poor Blacks as a theme were those respectable Blacks who deplored the increasing popularity of the *son* as a vulgar dance form which would bring them into disrepute. Although this criticism might seem misplaced, it was similar to that voiced by coloured American intellectuals such as W.E. Du Bois against McKay's novel *Home to Harlem,* in which he replicates Black speech and rhythms in depicting the life of poor Blacks. For Du Bois, as for the respectable members of Havana's Club Ateneo, Guillén was pandering to white stereotypes of Black behaviour.

Nothing daunted, Guillén published his next collection, *Sóngoro Cosongo* (1931), where his vision expands to cover more general black themes as in 'Sugar Cane' (p.23) where in only eight lines he goes to the heart of the brutal cropping of sugar. In *West Indies Ltd.* (1934) the tone is more combative as he extends his critique of imperialism to the Caribbean as a whole but once again, as in 'Guadeloupe' (p.49), he incorporates the essentials of that society in a few lines. Two poems in this collection deserve comment. In 'Sensemayá' (p.35) he employs *jitanjáfora,* an onomatopaic device, frequently used by negrista poets for whom it may often have been no more than a form of sonorous nonsense poetry. For Guillén, however, the words must be placed in a deeper African context. He uses them for sonority and rhythm, but at the same time there is an ancestral resonance in what is known as 'drum poetry', as in his *Canto Negro:*

Mamatomba, cuserembe, suserema,
tamba, tamba, tamba,
tamba, tamba, tamba,
tamba del negro que tumba.
Tumba del negro caramba.
Caramba que el negro tumba
yamba, yambo, yambambé.

The second poem 'Ballad of the Two Grandfathers' (p.27) one white, one black, goes to the heart of his *mulatez*, integrationist belief:

16

los dos del mismo tamaño
ansia negra, ansia blanca

He repudiates the notion that he is a poet of négritude, comparable to Aimé Césaire who had to fight against the assimilation of French cultural imperialism. 'We have discrimination in work, in hotels, in restaurants... I don't want to create one discrimination more, I am searching for a national poetry'. He regarded himself as an Afro-Latin, a poet of *mulatez*, a fusing of African and Spanish tradition in *cubanidad.* Hence the importance of Federico García Lorca, whom he met in Havana in the Spring of 1930.

If Hughes provided the link with American Blacks and their blues, with which Guillén compared his own work, Lorca was his link to the *madre-patria* of Spain. Lorca was captivated by Cuba after the cold impersonality of New York which he had just left, but where he had responded to the vigorous life of Harlem, and as a tribute to Cuba he composed his own *son* which he compared with his own fascination for the *romance*. This traditional popular ballad form had been revived by Lorca and was to be used to great effect during the Spanish Civil War, as Guillén discovered when he went to Spain in 1937 but by then, however, Lorca had been executed and was mourned in one of his poems from the collection *España* (p.61). While in Mexico, where he had gone for a conference, Guillén published his third collection, *Cantos para soldados y sones para turistas* in which his critique broadens further to include the whole of Latin America. It is dedicated to 'my father killed by soldiers' and there are echoes of the militarism which had ravaged Mexico. 'Execution' (p.55) reflects the iconography of the firing squad, a common theme of Mexican print makers which will have had echoes for Guillén of Batista's suppression of all opposition after he came to power in Cuba in 1934.

In mid 1937 he left Mexico with Octavio Paz, travelling for the only time through the United States in order to take a ship from Canada to attend the Congress of Writers for the Defence of Culture in Spain, to which he had been invited by Pablo Neruda. While there, he wrote articles for the Havana left wing journal *Mediodía* of which he was a member of the editorial board. He also joined the Communist Party (already influenced by the Spanish communist poet Rafael Alberti whom he had met in Havana the previous year). He also again met Langston Hughes who was covering the participation of American Blacks in the civil war. Their involvement in the struggle against fascism underlines an aspect of the war which is overlooked in the standard histories. For Blacks, the struggle against fascism, with its inherent racism, was being fought out in Abyssinia as well as in Spain where Italians were an integral part of Franco's army. Spain was therefore just a part of a much wider anti-colonial, anti-racist struggle, a view which the European Left was reluctant to recognize as it would have meant supporting a feudal regime in Abyssinia. Nothing better illustrates the gulf between the eurocentrism of the European left and the racial consciousness of radical Blacks than their respective attitudes to the Spanish and Abyssinian wars. The European left analysed the conflicts in European-derived class terms; in the Caribbean in particular, Haile Selassie's leadership of the anti-colonial struggle was interpreted in racial and religious ways, Selassie being seen as a god – the inspiration for Rastafarianism. The Spanish Civil War presaged the dilemma of choice between the universalism of Communism and the specificities of race. The war further internationalised Guillén's outlook, strengthening his anti-imperialist convictions which were to reach their apotheosis with the success of the Cuban Revolution.

On his return to Cuba in 1938 he became an editor of *Hoy*, the communist daily which Batista had legalized. He had now moved away from the apoliticism of his early years at Havana University – a rarity for a student at that time – to total commitment in the cause of social revolution, anti-racism and anti-imperialism. From now on his poetry is increasingly combative, for example in *Elegías* (1948-58) and *La paloma del vuelo popular (1958)*. Themes explored and hinted at in his earlier volumes come to ideological fruition in total commitment to revolutionary change. His anger is directed against racial crimes in 'Elegy for Emmett Till' (p.89), in 'It's all right' (p.133), in 'Governor' (p.137) and in 'Pupils' (p.137). In the 'Elegy for Jesus Menéndez', perhaps his most impressive poem, (but too long to be included here) the assassination of a popular black leader of Cuban sugar workers is described. Menéndez is again mentioned in 'I came on a slave ship' (p.129). In his last collection *La Rueda Dentada* (1972), episodes from the Cuban Revolution are recalled as in the two poems here 'Che Comandante' (p.169) and 'Guitarra en Duelo Mayor' (p.175).

On his return to Cuba in 1958 from exile during Batista's dictatorship in the 1950s, much of which was spent in Paris, he was soon recognized as the poet of the Revolution, travelling the world as a cultural diplomat. Increasingly, his duties as President of the Union of Cuban Writers and Artists (UNEAC) constricted his poetical activity, leaving him little time for poetical innovation apart from *El Diario que a Diario* (1972) which is not, as may appear on first sight simply a collage of pieces from the Cuban press but a radical experiment in exploring and analysing the nation's history. In many ways it was his most ambitious and original poem. "After this radical experiment" comments Antonio Benítez Rojo, "there was little left for Guillén to do".

Much of his later years were spent as roving ambassador for the Revolution, travelling the world and reading his poems as they were meant to be read in the oral traditions of African culture and of the Spanish ballad. He had been awarded the Lenin Peace Prize in 1954 but, although proposed, he did not win the Nobel Prize – that was to go to his rival, the other giant of Spanish American poetry, Pablo Neruda.

It is difficult to do justice to the immense wealth of Guillén's poetic range in a short selection – the deep resonances, the universal as well as the particular themes of his verses, the anger, pathos, musicality and the gamut of emotions, but the poems here, sensitively translated by Salvador Ortiz-Carboneres, have fanned the embers of enthusiasm and curiosity among even the unenthusiastic and incurious. They should encourage those who already know Spanish to go to the original collections and those who have still to learn to hasten to do so. To read Guillén and, through his poetry, to enter a world as ancestral, varied, controversial and challenging as he can conjure, is an excellent incentive to persevere in mastering the original Spanish.

RELOJ

Me gustan ciertas horas, como las 3 menos cuarto,
porque el reloj parece que tiene
una actitud fraterna, acogedora,
como si fuera a darnos un abrazo.

El tiempo, así, es un Cristo en agonía
que por la herida del costado
va desangrándose sutilmente
entre el Futuro y el Pasado.

THE CLOCK

I enjoy certain hours, like a quarter to three,
because the clock seems to hold
the warm friendliness of a brother
almost ready to embrace you.

Time, too, is a Christ in agony
bleeding gently
from the wound in his side
between the Future and the Past.

Poemas de Transición (1927-1931)

SÓNGORO
COSONGO

(1931)

CAÑA

El negro
junto al cañaveral.

El yanqui
sobre el cañaveral.

La tierra
bajo el cañaveral.

¡Sangre
que se nos va!

SUGARCANE

The Negro
bound to the canefield.

The Yankee
above the canefield.

The earth
beneath the canefield.

Blood
seeps out of us!

WEST INDIES, LTD.

1934

BALADA DE LOS DOS ABUELOS

Sombras que sólo yo veo,
me escoltan mis dos abuelos.

Lanza con punta de hueso,
tambor de cuero y madera:
mi abuelo negro.
Gorguera en el cuello ancho,
gris armadura guerrera:
mi abuelo blanco.

Pie desnudo, torso pétreo
los de mi negro;
pupilas de vidrio antártico
las de mi blanco!

África de selvas húmedas
y de gordos gongos sordos...
— ¡Me muero!
(Dice mi abuelo negro.)
Aguaprieta de caimanes,
verdes mañanas de cocos...
— ¡Me canso!
(Dice mi abuelo blanco.)
Oh velas de amargo viento,
galeón ardiendo en oro...
— ¡Me muero!
(Dice mi abuelo negro.)
¡Oh costas de cuello virgen
engañadas de abalorios...!
— ¡Me canso!
(Dice mi abuelo blanco.)
¡Oh puro sol repujado,
preso en el aro del trópico;
oh luna redonda y limpia
sobre el sueño de los monos!

BALLAD OF THE TWO GRANDFATHERS

Shadows that only I can see,
guarded by my two grandfathers.

A bone-point spear,
wood and hide drum:
my black grandfather.
A ruff round his broad neck,
a warrior's grey armour:
my white grandfather.

Bare feet, hardened body
had the black one;
pupils of antarctic glass
had the white one!

Africa of the humid jungles,
pounding and drumming gongs...
"I am dying!"
(says black grandfather.)
Swarthy alligator waters,
green coconut mornings....
"I tire!"
(says white grandfather.)
Ships of bitter wind,
galleon burning for gold...
"I am dying!"
(says black grandfather.)
Coastlines of virgin necks
beguiled in glass beads...!
"I tire!"
(says white grandfather.)
Pure circle of sun,
caught in the Tropic's ring;
clear round moon
over the sleeping apes!

¡Qué de barcos, qué de barcos!
¡Qué de negros, qué de negros!
¡Qué largo fulgor de cañas!
¡Qué látigo el del negrero!
Piedra de llanto y de sangre,
venas y ojos entreabiertos,
y madrugadas vacías,
y atardeceres de ingenio,
y una gran voz, fuerte voz,
despedazando el silencio.
¡Qué de barcos, qué de barcos,
qué de negros!

Sombras que sólo yo veo,
me escoltan mis dos abuelos.

Don Federico me grita
y Taita Facundo calla;
los dos en la noche sueñan
y andan, andan.
Yo los junto.

            — ¡Federico!
¡Facundo! Los dos se abrazan.
Los dos suspiran. Los dos
las fuertes cabezas alzan;
los dos del mismo tamaño,
bajo las estrellas altas;
los dos del mismo tamaño,
ansia negra y ansia blanca,
los dos del mismo tamaño,
gritan, sueñan, lloran, cantan.
Sueñan, lloran, cantan.
Lloran, cantan.
¡Cantan!

So many ships, so many ships!
So many Blacks, so many Blacks!
Such a splendour of sugarcane!
Such vigour in the slave-driver's whip!
Stone of tears and blood,
half-open eyes and veins,
empty dawns,
plantation sunsets,
and one strong loud voice,
cracking the silence.
So many ships, so many ships!
So many Blacks!

Shadows that only I can see,
guarded by my two grandfathers.

Don Federico bawls at me,
Taita[1]Facundo says nothing;
they dream in the night
going on, on....
I bring them together.

　　　"Federico!
Facundo!" They embrace.
They both sigh. They both
raise their strong heads;
two men of equal size,
under the lofty stars;
two men of equal size,
black and white longings,
two men of equal size,
they shout, dream, weep, sing.
They dream, weep, sing.
They weep, sing.
They sing!

BALADA DEL GÜIJE

¡Ñeque, que se vaya el ñeque!
¡Güije, que se vaya el güije!

Las turbias aguas del río
son hondas y tienen muertos;
carapachos de tortuga,
cabezas de niños negros.
De noche saca sus brazos
el río, y rasga el silencio
con sus uñas, que son uñas
de cocodrilo frenético.
Bajo el grito de los astros,
bajo una luna de incendio,
ladra el río entre las piedras
y con invisibles dedos,
sacude el arco del puente
y estrangula a los viajeros.

¡Ñeque, que se vaya el ñeque!
¡Güije, que se vaya el güije!

Enanos de ombligo enorme
pueblan las aguas inquietas;
sus cortas piernas, torcidas;
sus largas orejas, rectas.
¡Ah, que se comen mi niño,
de carnes puras y negras,
y que le beben la sangre,
y que le chupan las venas,
y que le cierran los ojos,
los grandes ojos de perlas!
¡Huye, que el coco te mata,
huye antes que el coco venga!
Mi chiquitín, chiquitón,
que tu collar te proteja...

BALLAD OF THE GÜIJE[2]

Ñeque[3], go away ñeque!
Güije, go away güije!

The river's murky waters
are deep and full of corpses;
turtle shells,
heads of black children.
By night the river flings out
its arms, and tears the silence
with its claws, claws
of a frantic crocodile.
Beneath the scream of the stars,
beneath a burning moon,
the river howls amongst the stones
and with invisible fingers,
shakes the bow of the bridge
and strangles travellers.

Ñeque, go away ñeque!
Güije, go away güije!

Dwarfs with huge navels
people the troubled waters;
their short legs twisted;
their huge ears, alert.
They are about to eat my child,
with his pure and black flesh,
and to drink his blood,
and suck on his veins,
and close his eyes,
his great eyes of pearl!
Run, the bogey-man will get you,
run before he comes!
My little boy, my little one,
may your lucky charm protect you...

Ñeque, que se vaya el ñeque!
¡Güije, que se vaya el güije!

Pero Changó no lo quiso.
Salió del agua una mano
para arrastrarlo...
Era un güije.
Le abrió en dos tapas el cráneo,
le apagó los grandes ojos,
le arrancó los dientes blancos,
e hizo un nudo con las piernas
y otro nudo con los brazos.

Mi chiquitín, chiquitón,
sonrisa de gordos labios,
con el fondo de tu río
está mi pena soñando,
y con tus venitas secas
y tu corazón mojado...
¡Ñeque, que se vaya el ñeque!
¡Güije, que se vaya el güije!
¡Ah, chiquitín, chiquitón,
pasó lo que yo te dije!

Ñeque, go away ñeque!
Güije, go away güije!

But Changó[4] didn't want that.
A hand came from the water
to drag him under.
It was a güije.
He split in two his skull,
tore out his huge eyes,
pulled out his white teeth,
tied his legs into one knot
and his arms into another.

My little boy, my little one,
with wide smiling lips,
my grief goes on dreaming
in the depths of your river
with your sweet dry veins
and your dampened heart...
Ñeque, go away ñeque!
Güije, go away güije!
My little boy, my little one,
all I told you came true!

SENSEMAYÁ

Canto para matar a una culebra.

¡Mayombe – bombe – mayombé!
¡Mayombe – bombe – mayombé!
¡Mayombe – bombe – mayombé!

La culebra tiene los ojos de vidrio;
la culebra viene y se enreda en un palo;
con sus ojos de vidrio, en un palo,
con sus ojos de vidrio.

La culebra camina sin patas;
la culebra se esconde en la yerba;
caminando se esconde en la yerba,
caminando sin patas.

¡Mayombe – bombe – mayombé!
¡Mayombe – bombe – mayombé!
¡Mayombe – bombe – mayombé!

Tú le das con el hacha y se muere:
¡dale ya!
¡No le des con el pie, que te muerde,
no le des con el pie, que se va!

Sensemayá, la culebra,
sensemayá.
Sensemayá, con sus ojos,
sensemayá.
Sensemayá, con su lengua,
sensemayá.
Sensemayá, con su boca,
sensemayá.

SENSEMAYÁ

Chant for killing a small snake

¡Mayombe – bombe – mayombé![5]
¡Mayombe – bombe – mayombé!
¡Mayombe – bombe – mayombé!

The small snake has eyes of glass;
the small snake comes, curls round a stick;
with its eyes of glass, around a stick,
with its eyes of glass.

The small snake walks with no feet;
the small snake hides in the grass;
walking it hides in the grass,
walking with no feet.

¡Mayombe – bombe – mayombé!
¡Mayombe – bombe – mayombé!
¡Mayombe – bombe – mayombé!

You strike it with an axe and it dies:
strike it now!
Don't kick it with your foot, for it bites,
don't kick it with your foot, it will escape!

Sensemayá, the snake,
sensemayá.
Sensemayá, with its eyes,
sensemayá.
Sensemayá, with its tongue,
sensemayá.
Sensemayá, with its mouth,
sensemayá.

La culebra muerta no puede comer,
la culebra muerta no puede silbar,
no puede caminar,
no puede correr.

La culebra muerta no puede mirar,
la culebra muerta no puede beber,
no puede respirar
no puede morder.

¡Mayombe – bombe – mayombé!
Sensemayá, la culebra...
¡Mayombe – bombe – mayombé!
Sensemayá, no se mueve...
¡Mayombe – bombe – mayombé!
Sensemayá, la culebra...
¡Mayombe – bombe – mayombé!
Sensemayá, se murió.

The dead snake can't eat,
the dead snake can't hiss,
can't walk,
can't run.

The dead snake can't see
the dead snake can't drink,
can't breathe,
can't bite.

¡Mayombe – bombe – mayombé!
Sensemayá, the small snake...
¡Mayombe – bombe – mayombé!
Sensemayá, it doesn't move...
¡Mayombe – bombe – mayombé!
Sensemayá, the small snake...
¡Mayombe – bombe – mayombé!
Sensemayá, the snake is dead.

EL ABUELO

Esta mujer angélica de ojos septentrionales,
que vive atenta al ritmo de su sangre europea,
ignora que en lo hondo de ese ritmo golpea
un negro el parche duro de roncos atabales.

Bajo la línea escueta de su nariz aguda,
la boca, en fino trazo, traza una raya breve,
y no hay cuervo que manche la solitaria nieve
de su carne, que fulge temblorosa y desnuda.

¡Ah, mi señora! Mírate las venas misteriosas;
boga en el agua viva que allá dentro te fluye,
 y ve pasando lirios, nelumbios, lotos, rosas;

que ya verás, inquieta, junto a la fresca orilla
la dulce sombra oscura del abuelo que huye,
el que rizó por siempre tu cabeza amarilla.

THE GRANDFATHER

The angelic woman with her northern eyes,
lives close to the rhythm of her European blood
not knowing that in the depths of that rhythm
a Black beats hard on a harsh sounding drum.

Under the sharp line of her aquiline nose,
her fine mouth is drawn in a short line,
and no raven darkens the virgin snow
of her flesh, that quivers naked and gleaming.

Oh, my lady! Look at your mysterious veins;
row in the live waters that flow deep within you,
and see in passing, lilies, nelumbos[6], lotuses, roses;

soon your troubled eyes will see, close to the calm shore,
the sweet dark shadow of your fleeing grandfather,
the one who kinked for ever your yellow hair.

6

¡West Indies! ¡West Indies! ¡West Indies!
Éste es el pueblo hirsuto,
de cobre, multicéfalo donde la vida repta
con el lodo seco cuarteado en la piel.
Éste es el presidio
donde cada hombre tiene atados los pies.
Ésta es la grotesca sede de companies y trusts.
Aquí están el lago de asfalto, las minas de hierro,
las plantaciones de café,
los ports docks, los ferry boats, los ten cents...
Éste es el pueblo del all right,
donde todo se encuentra muy mal;
éste es el pueblo del very well,
donde nadie está bien.

Aquí están los servidores de Mr. Babbit.
Los que educan sus hijos en West Point.
Aquí están los que chillan: hello baby,
y fuman «Chesterfield» y «Lucky Strike».
Aquí están los bailadores de fox trots,
los boys del jazz band
y los veraneantes de Miami y de Palm Beach.
Aquí están los que piden bread and butter
y coffee and milk.
Aquí están los absurdos jóvenes sifilíticos,
fumadores de opio y de mariguana,
exhibiendo en vitrinas sus espiroquetas
y cortándose un traje cada semana.
Aqui está lo mejor de Port-au-Prince,
lo más puro de Kingston, la high life de La Habana...
Pero aquí están también los que reman en lágrimas,
galeotes dramáticos, galeotes dramáticos.

WEST INDIES, LTD.

6

West Indies! West Indies! West Indies!
These are the rough people,
of copper, multicephalous[7], where life crawls
with the dry mud cracked on the skin.
This is the prison
where each man's feet are tied.
This is the grotesque head office of companies and trusts.
Here are the asphalt lake, the iron mines,
the coffee plantations,
the ports' docks, the ferry boats, the ten cents...
These are the people who say 'all right',
where everything is very bad for them;
these are the people who say 'very well',
where no one is well.

Here are Mr Babbit's[8] servants.
Those who educate their children at West Point.
Here are those who shout: 'hello baby',
and smoke Chesterfield and Lucky Strike.
Here are the foxtrot dancers,
the boys of the jazz band
and the summer tourists from Miami and Palm Beach.
Here are those who ask for bread and butter
and coffee and milk.
Here are the ludicrous syphilitic youths,
smokers of opium and marijuana,
openly displaying their sores,
and having themselves a new suit made each week.
Here is the cream of Port-au-Prince,
the purest of Kingston, the high life of Havana...
But here are also those who row in tears,
dramatic galleys, dramatic galleys.

Aquí están ellos,
los que trabajan con un haz de destellos
la piedra dura donde poco a poco se crispa
el puño de un titán. Los que encienden la chispa
roja, sobre el campo reseco.
Los que gritan: «¡Ya vamos!», y les responde el eco
de otras voces: «¡Ya vamos!» Los que en fiero tumulto
sienten latir la sangre con sílabas de insulto.
¿Qué hacer con ellos,
si trabajan con un haz de destellos?

Aquí están los que codo con codo
todo lo arriesgan; todo
lo dan con generosas manos;
aquí están los que se sienten hermanos
del negro, que doblando sobre el zanjón oscuro
la frente, se disuelve en sudor puro,
y del blanco, que sabe que la carne es arcilla
mala cuando la hiere el látigo, y peor si se la humilla
bajo la bota, porque entonces levanta
la voz, que es como un trueno brutal en la garganta.
Ésos son los que sueñan despiertos,
los que en el fondo de la mina luchan,
y allí la voz escuchan
con que gritan los vivos y los muertos.

Ésos, los iluminados,
los parias desconocidos,
los humillados,
los preteridos,
los olvidados,
los descosidos,
los amarrados,
los ateridos,
los que ante el máuser exclaman:
  ««¡Hermanos soldados!»»
y ruedan heridos

They are here,
those who work with a sheaf of sparkling rays
the hard stone where, little by little,
a Titon's fist will clench. Those who light
the red spark, on the dried up field.
Those who shout: 'We are coming', and are answered
by echoing voices: 'We are coming'. Those who in
wild uproar feel their blood beat with words of contempt.
What should be done with them,
if they work with a sheaf of sparkling rays?

Here are those who shoulder to shoulder
risk everything; all,
they give with generous hands;
here are those who feel themselves brothers
of the Black, who bending his head
over the dark ditch, dissolves into pure sweat,
and of the White, who knows that flesh is defective clay
when the whip lashes it, and worse if it is trodden
beneath the boot, because then the voice rises
like a brutal thunderclap in the throat.
These are the people who dream while waking,
those who fight in the heart of the mine
where they listen to voices,
the cries of the living and the dead.

These are the enlightened ones,
the unknown outcasts,
the humiliated,
the ignored,
the forgotten,
the uprooted,
the enchained,
the numbed,
those who when faced with a Mauser[9] say:
'Brother soldiers!'
and roll wounded

con un hilo rojo en los labios morados.
(¡Que siga su marcha el tumulto!
¡Que floten las bárbaras banderas,
y que se enciendan las banderas
sobre el tumulto!)

7
Cinco minutos de interrupción.
La charanga de Juan el Barbero
toca un son.

— Me matan, si no trabajo,
y si trabajo, me matan;
siempre me matan, me matan,
siempre me matan.

Ayer vi a un hombre mirando,
mirando el sol que salía;
ayer vi a un hombre mirando,
mirando el sol que salía:
el hombre estaba muy serio,
porque el hombre no veía.
Ay,
los ciegos viven sin ver
cuando sale el sol,
cuando sale el sol,
¡cuando sale el sol!

Ayer vi a un niño jugando
a que mataba a otro niño;
ayer vi a un niño jugando
a que mataba a otro niño:
hay niños que se parecen
a los hombres trabajando.
¡Quién les dirá cuando crezcan
que los hombres no son niños,

with a red thread on their purple lips.
(May the uproar march on!
May the daring flags fly,
and may the flags catch fire
over the uproar!)

7
Five minutes interruption.
Juan the Barber's brass band
plays a tune.

They'll kill me, if I don't work,
and if I do, they'll still kill me;
they go on killing me,
killing me, killing me.

Yesterday I saw a man pondering,
contemplating the rising sun;
yesterday I saw a man pondering,
contemplating the rising sun:
the man was extremely serious,
because the man couldn't see.
Alas,
blind men live without seeing
the sunrise,
the sunrise,
the sunrise!

Yesterday I saw a child in a game
killing another child;
yesterday I saw a child in a game
killing another child:
there are children who look
like men at work.
Who will tell them when they grow up
that men aren't children,

que no lo son,
que no lo son,
que no lo son!

Me matan, si no trabajo,
y si trabajo, me matan:
siempre me matan, me matan,
¡siempre me matan!

they are no more,
they are no more,
they are no more!

They'll kill me, if I don't work,
and if I do, they'll still kill me:
they go on killing me,
killing me, killing me!

GUADALUPE W.I.

POINTE-À-PITRE

Los negros, trabajando
junto al vapor. Los árabes, vendiendo,
los franceses, paseando y descansando,
y el sol, ardiendo. . .

En el puerto se acuesta
el mar. El aire tuesta
las palmeras. . . Yo grito: ¡Guadalupe!, pero nadie contesta,

Parte el vapor, arando
las aguas impasibles con espumoso estruendo.
Allá, quedan los negros trabajando,
los árabes vendiendo,
los franceses paseando y descansando,
y el sol ardiendo...

GUADELOUPE, W.I.

POINTE-À-PITRE

The Blacks, working
near the ship. The Arabs, selling,
the French, strolling and relaxing,
and the sun, blazing...

In the harbour, the sea
goes into port to sleep. The air scorches
the palm trees. . . I shout: Guadeloupe! but nobody answers.

The ship weighs anchor, ploughing
the impassive waters with foaming clamour.
The Blacks stay behind working,
the Arabs selling,
the French strolling and relaxing
and the sun, blazing...

CANTOS PARA SOLDADOS
Y SONES PARA TURISTAS

(1937)

NO SÉ POR QUÉ PIENSAS TÚ

No sé por qué piensas tú,
soldado, que te odio yo;
si somos la misma cosa
yo,
tú.

Tú eres pobre, lo soy yo;
soy de abajo, lo eres tú;
¿de dónde has sacado tú,
soldado, que te odio yo?

Me duele que a veces tú
te olvides de quién soy yo;
caramba, si yo soy tú,
lo mismo que tú eres yo.

Pero no por eso yo
he de malquererte, tú;
si somos la misma cosa,
yo,
tú,
no sé por qué piensas tú,
soldado, que te odio yo.

Ya nos veremos yo y tú,
juntos en la misma calle,
hombro con hombro, tú y yo,
sin odios ni yo ni tú,
pero sabiendo tú y yo,
a dónde vamos yo y tú...
¡No sé por qué piensas tú,
soldado, que te odio yo!

I DON'T KNOW WHY YOU THINK

I don't know why you think,
soldier, that I hate you;
if we are exactly the same,
I,
you.

You are poor, so am I;
I am an underdog, so are you;
where did you get the idea,
soldier, that I hate you?

It hurts me at times that you
forget who I am;
Jesus, if I am you
just as you are me.

But not for that, do I
bear ill will towards you;
if we are both the same
I,
you.
I don't know why you think,
soldier, that I hate you.

We'll soon meet, you and I,
together in the same street,
shoulder to shoulder, you and I,
without hatred, neither I nor you,
but knowing you and I,
where we are going, I and you...
I don't know why you think,
soldier, that I hate you!

FUSILAMIENTO

Van a fusilar
a un hombre que tiene los brazos atados.
Hay cuatro soldados
para disparar.
Son cuatro soldados
callados,
que están amarrados,
lo mismo que el hombre amarrado que van
a matar.

— ¿Puedes escapar?
— ¡No puedo correr!
— ¡Ya van a tirar!
— ¡Qué vamos a hacer!
— Quizá los rifles no estén cargados...
— ¡Seis balas tienen de fiero plomo!
— ¡Quizá no tiren esos soldados!
— ¡Eres un tonto de tomo y lomo!

Tiraron.
(¿Cómo fue que pudieron tirar?)
Mataron.
(¿Cómo fue que pudieron matar?)
Eran cuatro soldados
callados,
y les hizo una seña, bajando su sable,
un señor oficial;
eran cuatro soldados
atados,
lo mismo que el hombre que fueron
los cuatro a matar.

EXECUTION

They are going to shoot
a man whose arms are bound.
There are four soldiers
in the firing squad.
They are four soldiers
silent,
who are trapped,
just like the man, they are going
to kill.

"Can you escape?"
"I can't run!"
"They're going to fire!"
"What can we do!"
"The rifles might not be loaded..."
"They have six bullets of terrible lead!"
"The soldiers might not shoot!"
"You are such a fool!"

They fired.
(How could they fire?)
They killed.
(How could they kill?)
They were four soldiers
silent,
and an officer, lowering his sword,
gave the order;
they were four soldiers
bound,
just like the man the four had gone
to kill.

SOLDADO LIBRE

¡Ya no volveré al cuartel,
suelto por calles y plazas,
yo mismo, Pedro Cortés!

Yo mismo dueño de mí,
ya por fin libre de guardias,
de uniforme y de fusil.

Podré a mi pueblo correr,
y gritar, cuando me vean:
¡aquí está Pedro Cortés!

Podré trabajar al sol,
y en la tierra que me espera,
con mi arado labrador.

Ser hombre otra vez de paz,
cargar niños, besar frentes,
cantar, reír y saltar.

¡Ya no volveré al cuartel,
suelto por calles y plazas,
yo mismo, Pedro Cortés!

FREE SOLDIER

I'll never go back to the barracks,
free in squares and streets,
I am myself, Pedro Cortés!

I, my own master,
now at last free from guard duties,
from uniforms and rifles.

I will be able to run to my town
and to shout, when they see me:
here is Pedro Cortés!

I will be able to work in the sun,
and on the land, which is waiting for me,
with my industrious plough.

Being a man of peace again,
carrying children, kissing foreheads,
singing, laughing, leaping.

I'll never go back to the barracks,
free in squares and streets,
I am myself, Pedro Cortés!

ESPAÑA

POEMA EN CUATRO ANGUSTIAS
Y UNA ESPERANZA

(1937)

ANGUSTIA CUARTA

Federico

Toco a la puerta de un romance.
— ¿No anda por aquí Federico?
Un papagayo me contesta:
— Ha salido.

Toco a una puerta de cristal.
— ¿No anda por aquí Federico?
Viene una mano y me señala:
— Está en el río.

Toco a la puerta de un gitano.
— ¿No anda por aquí Federico?
Nadie responde, no habla nadie...
— ¡Federico! ¡Federico!

La casa oscura, vacía;
negro musgo en las paredes;
brocal de pozo sin cubo,
jardín de lagartos verdes.

Sobre la tierra mullida
caracoles que se mueven,
y el rojo viento de julio
entre las ruinas, meciéndose.

¡Federico!
¿Dónde el gitano se muere?
¿Dónde sus ojos se enfrían?
¡Dónde estará, que no viene!

FOURTH SORROW

Federico[10]

I knock at the door of Romance.
"Is Federico around?"
A parrot answers me:
"He went out."

I knock at a glass door.
"Is Federico around?"
A hand gestures to me:
"He is in the river."

I knock at a gypsy's door.
"Is Federico around?"
Nobody answers, nobody speaks...
"Federico!" "Federico!"

The house dark, empty;
black moss on the walls;
the lip of the well has no bucket,
a garden of green lizards.

On the freshly turned earth
the snails are moving,
the red July wind
lingers among the ruins.

Federico!
Where does the gypsy die?
Where do his eyes turn cold?
Where can he be, for he is not coming!

EL SON ENTERO

(1947)

SUDOR Y LÁTIGO

Látigo,
sudor y látigo.

El sol despertó temprano
y encontró al negro descalzo,
desnudo el cuerpo llagado,
sobre el campo.

Látigo,
sudor y látigo.

El viento pasó gritando:
– ¡Qué flor negra en cada mano!
La sangre le dijo: ¡vamos!
Él dijo a la sangre: ¡vamos!
Partió en su sangre, descalzo.
El cañaveral, temblando,
le abrió paso.

Después, el cielo callado,
y bajo el cielo, el esclavo
tinto en la sangre del amo.

Látigo,
sudor y látigo,
tinto en la sangre del amo;
látigo,
sudor y látigo,
tinto en la sangre del amo,
tinto en la sangre del amo.

SWEAT AND WHIP

Whip,
sweat and whip.

The sun rose early
and found the barefoot Black,
in the field
body naked and scarred.

Whip,
sweat and whip.

The wind went by screaming:
Black flowers in every hand!
His blood said to him: let's go!
He said to his blood: let's go!
He left, barefoot and bleeding.
The canefield, trembling,
let him pass.

Later, the silent sky,
beneath the sky, the slave
stained with the master's blood.

Whip,
sweat and whip,
stained with the master's blood;
whip,
sweat and whip,
stained with the master's blood,
stained with the master's blood.

SON NÚMERO 6

Yoruba soy, lloro en yoruba
lucumí.
Como soy un yoruba de Cuba,
quiero que hasta Cuba suba mi llanto yoruba,
que suba el alegre llanto yoruba
que sale de mí.

Yoruba soy,
cantando voy,
llorando estoy,
y cuando no soy yoruba,
soy congo, mandinga, carabalí.
Atiendan, amigos, mi son, que empieza así:

Adivinanza
de la esperanza:
lo mío es tuyo,
lo tuyo es mío;
toda la sangre
formando un río.

La ceiba ceiba con su penacho;
el padre padre con su muchacho;
la jicotea en su carapacho.
¡Que rompa el son caliente,
y que lo baile la gente,
pecho con pecho,
vaso con vaso
y agua con agua con aguardiente!
Yoruba soy, soy lucumí,
mandinga, congo, carabalí.
Atiendan, amigos, mi son, que sigue así:

Estamos juntos desde muy lejos,
jóvenes, viejos,

SON[11] NUMBER 6

I'm Yoruba, crying out Yoruba[12]
Lucumí.
Since I'm Yoruba from Cuba,
I want my lament of Yoruba to touch Cuba
the joyful weeping Yoruba
that comes out of me.

I'm Yoruba,
I keep singing
and crying.
When not Yoruba
I am Congo, Mandinga or Carabalí.
Listen my friends, to my *'son'* which begins like this:

Here is the riddle
of all my hopes:
what's mine is yours,
what's yours is mine;
all the blood
shaping a river.

The silk-cotton tree, tree with its crown;
father, the father with his son;
the tortoise in its shell.
Let the heart-warming *'son'* break out,
and our people dance,
heart close to heart,
glasses clinking together
water on water with rum!
I'm Yoruba, I'm Lucumí,
Mandinga, Congo, Carabalí.
Listen my friends, to the *'son'* that goes like this:

We've come together from far away,
young ones and old,

negros y blancos, todo mezclado;
uno mandando y otro mandado,
todo mezclado;
San Berenito y otro mandado,
todo mezclado;
negros y blancos desde muy lejos,
todo mezclado;
Santa María y uno mandado,
todo mezclado;
todo mezclado, Santa María,
San Berenito, todo mezclado,
todo mezclado, San Berenito,
San Berenito, Santa María,
Santa María, San Berenito,
¡todo mezclado!

Yoruba soy, soy lucumí,
mandinga, congo, carabalí.
Atiendan, amigos, mi son, que acaba así:

      Salga el mulato,
      suelte el zapato,
      díganle al blanco que no se va...
      De aquí no hay nadie que se separe;
      mire y no pare,
      oiga y no pare,
      beba y no pare,
      coma y no pare,
      viva y no pare,
      ¡que el son de todos no va a parar!

Blacks and Whites, moving together;
one is a leader, the other a follower,
all moving together;
San Berenito and one who's obeying
all moving together;
Blacks and Whites from far away,
all moving together;
Santa María and one who's obeying
all moving together;
all pulling together, Santa María,
San Berenito, all pulling together,
all moving together, San Berenito,
San Berenito, Santa María.
Santa María, San Berenito,
everyone pulling together!

I'm Yoruba, I'm Lucumí
Mandinga, Congo, Carabalí.
Listen my friends, to my *'son'* which ends like this:

> Come out Mulatto,
> walk on free,
> tell the white man he can't leave...
> Nobody breaks away from here;
> look and don't stop,
> listen and don't wait
> drink and don't stop,
> eat and don't wait,
> live and don't hold back
> our people's *'son'* will never end!

UN SON PARA NIÑOS ANTILLANOS

Por el Mar de las Antillas
anda un barco de papel:
anda y anda el barco barco,
sin timonel.

De La Habana a Portobelo,
de Jamaica a Trinidad,
anda y anda el barco barco,
sin capitán.

Una negra va en la popa,
va en la proa un español:
anda y anda el barco barco,
con ellos dos.

Pasan islas, islas, islas,
muchas islas, siempre más;
anda y anda el barco barco,
sin descansar.

Un cañón de chocolate
contra el barco disparó,
y un cañón de azúcar, azúcar,
le contestó.

¡Ay, mi barco marinero,
con su casco de papel!
¡Ay, mi barco negro y blanco
sin timonel!

Allá va la negra negra,
junto junto al español;
anda y anda el barco barco
con ellos dos.

SON FOR ANTILLIAN CHILDREN

Over the Antilles sea,
sails a paper boat:
the boat sails and sails,
with no helmsman.

From Havana to Portobelo,
from Jamaica to Trinidad,
the boat sails and sails,
with no captain.

A black woman is at the stern,
a Spaniard is at the prow:
the boat sails and sails,
with both of them aboard.

They pass islands, islands, islands,
many islands, more and more;
the boat sails and sails,
and does not stop.

A chocolate cannon,
fired against the boat,
and a sugar cannon,
sweetly replied.

Oh my sailing boat,
with its paper hull!
Oh my black and white boat
with no helmsman!

Over there sails the black, black woman,
close, close to the Spaniard;
the boat sails and sails
with both of them aboard.

POEMA CON NIÑOS

A Vicente Martínez

La escena, en un salón familiar. La madre, blanca, y su hijo. Un niño negro, uno chino, uno judío, que están de visita. Todos de doce años más o menos. La madre, sentada, hace labor, mientras a su lado, ellos juegan con unos soldaditos de plomo.

I

LA MADRE. *(Dirigiéndose al grupo.)* ¿No ven? Aquí están mejor que allá, en la calle... No sé cómo hay madres despreocupadas, que dejan a sus hijos solos todo el día por esos mundos de Dios. *(Se dirige al niño negro.)* Y tú, ¿cómo te llamas?

EL NEGRO. ¿Yo? Manuel. *(Señalando al chino.)* Y éste se llama Luis. *(Señalando al judío.)* Y éste se llama Jacobo...

LA MADRE. Oye, ¿sabes que estás enterado, eh? ¿Vives cerca de aquí?

EL NEGRO. ¿Yo? No, señora. *(Señalando al chino.)* Ni éste tampoco... *(Señalando al judío.)* Ni éste...

EL JUDÍO. Yo vivo por allá por la calle de Acosta, cerca de la Terminal. Mi papá es zapatero. Yo quiero ser médico. Tengo una hermanita que toca el piano, pero como en casa no hay piano, siempre va a casa de una amiga suya, que tiene un piano de cola... El otra día le dio un dolor...

LA MADRE. ¿Al piano de cola o a tu hermanita?

EL JUDÍO. *(Ríe.)* No; a la amiga de mi hermanita. Yo fui a buscar al doctor...

LA MADRE. ¡Anjá! Pero ya se curó, ¿verdad?

POEM WITH CHILDREN

To Vicente Martínez

A homely sitting room. The mother, a white woman and her son. A black boy, a Chinese[13] boy, a Jewish boy who are visiting. All of them are about 12 years old. The mother is sitting doing some needlework while next to her the children are playing with toy lead soldiers.

I

THE MOTHER *(Addressing the group)* Now then. Aren't you better off here than out in the street...? I don't know how some mothers can be so thoughtless as to allow their children to play alone all day in those God-forsaken places. *(Turning to the black boy.)* You, what's your name?

BLACK BOY. Me? Manuel. *(Pointing to the Chinese boy)* And he's Luis. *(Pointing to the Jewish boy.)* And he's Jacobo...

THE MOTHER. I see, you are well informed, aren't you? Do you live round here?

BLACK BOY. Me? No ma'am. *(Pointing to the Chinese boy)* Nor does he. *(Pointing to the Jewish boy.)* Nor him...

JEWISH BOY. I live over there by Acosta Street, near the Terminal. My father is a shoemaker. I want to be a Doctor. I have a little sister who plays the piano... but as we haven't got one... she always goes to her friend's house, who's got a grand piano... The other day something terrible happened...

THE MOTHER: To the grand piano or your little sister?

JEWISH BOY. *(Laughing)* No, my sister's friend. I went to fetch the Doctor...

THE MOTHER. Mmm. But she is better now, isn't she?

73

EL JUDÍO. Sí; se curó en seguida; no era un dolor muy fuerte...

LA MADRE. ¡Qué bueno! *(Dirigiéndose al niño chino.)* ¿Y tú? A ver, cuéntame. ¿Cómo te llamas tú?

EL CHINO. Luis...

LA MADRE. ¿Luis? Verdad, hombre, si hace un momento lo había chismeado el pícaro de Manuel... ¿Y qué, tú eres chino de China, Luis? ¿Tú sabes hablar en chino?

EL CHINO. No, señora; mi padre es chino, pero yo no soy chino. Yo soy cubano, y mi mamá también.

EL HIJO. ¡Mamá! ¡Mamá! *(Señalando al chino.)* El padre de éste tenía una fonda, y la vendió...

LA MADRE. ¿Sí? ¿Y cómo lo sabes tú, Rafaelito?

EL HIJO. *(Señalando al chino.)* Porque éste me lo dijo. ¿No es verdad, Luis?

EL CHINO. Verdad, yo se lo dije, porque mamá me lo contó.

LA MADRE. Bueno, a jugar, pero sin pleitos, ¿eh? No quiero disputas. Tú, Rafael, no te cojas los soldados para ti solo, y dales a ellos también...

EL HIJO. Sí, mamá, si ya se los repartí. Tocamos a seis cada uno. Ahora vamos a hacer una parada, porque los soldados se marchan a la guerra...

LA MADRE. Bueno, en paz, y no me llames, porque estoy por allá dentro... *(Vase)*

JEWISH BOY. Yes, she recovered in no time. It wasn't a very bad pain...

THE MOTHER. What a relief! *(Addressing the Chinese boy)* And you, come on tell me what's your name?

CHINESE BOY. Luis...

THE MOTHER. Luis? Yes that's it; a mischievious little bird called Manuel told me just now.... Where do you come from Luis, from China? Can you speak Chinese?

CHINESE BOY. No ma'am; my father is Chinese but I am not Chinese. I am Cuban and so is my mother

THE SON. Mum! Mum! *(Pointing to the Chinese boy)* His father used to have a restaurant. And he sold it...

THE MOTHER. Yes. And how do you know that, Rafaelito?

THE SON. *(Pointing to the Chinese boy)* Because he told me. Didn't you, Luis?

CHINESE BOY. Yes, I told him because mum told me.

THE MOTHER. Right, go and play now, but no arguing. I don't want any fights. You, Rafael, don't take all the soldiers, share them with your friends...

THE SON. Yes mum, I already have. We've got six each. We are going to have a parade because the soldiers are going to war...

THE MOTHER. Right, but quietly, and don't call me because I've got things to do inside. *(She leaves)*

II

Los niños, solos, hablan mientras juegan con sus soldaditos.

EL HIJO. Estos soldados me los regaló un capitán que vive ahí enfrente. Me los dio el día de mi santo.

EL NEGRO. Yo nunca he tenido soldaditos como los tuyos. Oye: ¿no te fijas en que todos son iguales?

EL JUDÍO. ¡Claro! Porque son de plomo. Pero los soldados de verdad...

EL HIJO. ¿Qué?

EL JUDÍO. ¡Pues que son distintos! Unos son altos y otros más pequeños. ¿Tú no ves que son hombres?

EL NEGRO. Sí, señor; los hombres son distintos. Unos son grandes, como éste dice, y otros son más chiquitos. Unos negros y otros blancos, y otros amarillos *(señalando al chino)* como éste... Mi maestra dijo en la clase el otro día que los negros son menos que los blancos... ¡A mí me dio una pena!...

EL JUDÍO. Sí... También un alemán que tiene una botica en la calle de Compostela me dijo que yo era un perro, y que a todos los de mi raza los debían matar. Yo no lo conozco ni nunca le hice nada. Y ni mi mamá ni mi papá tampoco... ¡Tenía más mal carácter!..

EL CHINO. A mí me dijo también la maestra, que la raza amarilla era menos que la blanca... La blanca es la mejor...

EL HIJO. Sí, yo lo leí en un libro que tengo: un libro de geografía. Pero dice mi mamá que eso es mentira; que todos los hombres y todos los niños son iguales. Yo no sé cómo va a ser, porque fíjate que ¿no ves? yo tengo la carne de un color, y tú *(se*

II

Left alone the children talk while they play with their
toy soldiers.

THE SON. These soldiers were a present to me from a Captain who lives opposite us. He gave them to me on my Saint's day.

BLACK BOY. I have never had any soldiers like yours. Hey! have you noticed that they're all the same?

JEWISH BOY. Of course! They are all made of lead. But real soldiers...

THE SON. What?

JEWISH BOY. Well they're all different! Some are tall and others are shorter. They are men, you see?

BLACK BOY. Yes man; men are different. Some are big, like he says, others are small. Some are black and others white, and others yellow *(pointing to the Chinese)* like him... In the class the other day my teacher said that there are more Whites than Blacks... That really hurt me!...

JEWISH BOY. Yes... And a German who has a drug store in Compostela Street called me a pig and said that all the people of my race should be killed. I don't know him and I never did him any harm. Neither did my father or my mother... He was really nasty!...

CHINESE BOY. My teacher told me too that the yellow race was inferior to the white... That the white is the best...

THE SON. Yes, I read that in my book: a geography book. But my mum says it's all a lie; that all people and all children are the same. I don't see how that is possible: well my skin is one colour

dirige al chino) de otro, y tú *(se dirige al negro)* de otro, y tú *(se dirige al judío)* y tú... ¡Pues mira qué cosa! ¡Tú no, tú eres blanco igual que yo!

EL JUDÍO. Es verdad; pero dicen que como tengo la nariz, así un poco... no sé... un poco larga, pues que soy menos que otras gentes que la tienen más corta. ¡Un lío! Yo me fijo en los hombres y en otros muchachos por ahí, que también tienen la nariz larga, y nadie les dice nada...

EL CHINO. ¡Porque son cubanos!

EL NEGRO. *(Dirigiéndose al chino.)* Sí... Tú también eres cubano, y tienes los ojos prendidos como los chinos...

EL CHINO. ¡Porque mi padre era chino, animal!

EL NEGRO. ¡Pues entonces tú no eres cubano! ¡Y no tienes que decirme animal! ¡Vete para Cantón!

EL CHINO. ¡Y tú, vete para Africa, negro!

EL HIJO. ¡No griten, que viene mamá, y luego va a pelear!

EL JUDÍO. ¿Pero tú no ves que este negro le dijo chino?

EL NEGRO ¡Cállate, tú, judío, perro, que tu padre es zapatero y tu familia...!

EL JUDÍO. Y tú, carbón de piedra, y tú, mono, y tú...

(Todos se enredan a golpes, con gran escándalo. Aparece la madre, corriendo.)

and yours *(to the Chinese)* is different, and yours *(to the Black)*, is different and yours *(to the Jew)* Well, how about that..., you are white like me!

JEWISH BOY. That's true: but they say that my nose, is... I don't know...a bit long, and because of that I am not as good as other people with shorter noses. Really confusing! I have seen men and other boys around here who have long noses too and no one says anything to them...

CHINESE BOY. Because they are Cubans!

BLACK BOY. *(Addressing the Chinese boy)* Yes, and so are you, but your eyes are slanted....

CHINESE BOY. Because my father was Chinese, stupid!

BLACK BOY. Then you are not Cuban! And don't call me stupid! Go back to Canton!

CHINESE BOY. And you nigger, go back to Africa.

THE SON. Don't shout, mum will come and tell us off!

JEWISH BOY. Didn't you hear this black kid called him Chinese?

BLACK BOY. Shut up you Jewish pig, son of a shoemaker and your family...!

JEWISH BOY. And you, you lump of coal, and you, ape, you...

(They all start fighting noisily. The Mother comes in running.)

III

LA MADRE. ¡Pero qué es eso! ¿Se han vuelto locos? ¡A ver, Rafaelito, ven aquí! ¿Qué es lo que pasa?

EL HIJO. Nada, mamá, que se pelearon por el color...

LA MADRE. ¿Cómo por el color? No te entiendo...

EL HIJO. Sí, te digo que por el color, mamá...

EL CHINO. *(Señalando al negro.)* ¡Señora, porque éste me dijo chino, y que me fuera para Cantón!

EL NEGRO. Sí, y tú me dijiste negro, y que me fuera para Africa...

LA MADRE. *(Riendo.)* ¡Pero, hombre! ¿Será posible? ¡Si todos son lo mismo!

EL JUDÍO. No, señora; yo no soy igual a un negro...

EL HIJO. ¿Tú ves, mamá, como es por el color?

EL NEGRO. Yo no soy igual a un chino...

EL CHINO. ¡Míralo! ¡Ni yo quiero ser igual a ti!

EL HIJO. ¿Tú ves, mamá, tú ves?

LA MADRE. *(Autoritariamente.)* ¡Silencio! ¡Sentarse y escuchar! *(Los niños obedecen, sentándose en el suelo, próximos a la madre, que comienza)*:

La sangre es un mar inmenso
que baña todas las playas...
Sobre sangre van los hombres,

III

THE MOTHER. What's going on here! Have you gone mad? Rafaelito come here! What's the matter with all of you?

THE SON. Nothing mum, they were fighting because of their colour...

THE MOTHER. Because of their colour? I don't understand...

THE SON. Yes mum, because of their colour...

CHINESE BOY. *(Pointing to the Black)* Ma'am, he called me Chinese and told me to go back to Canton.

BLACK BOY. Yes, and you called me nigger and told me to go back to Africa...

THE MOTHER. *(Laughing)* But boys. I can't believe it! You are all the same.

JEWISH BOY. No, ma'am. I don't look like a nigger...

THE SON. You see mum, it's all to do with colour.

BLACK BOY. I don't look like a Chinese...

CHINESE BOY. Look at him! I don't want to look like you!

THE SON. See mum? See?

THE MOTHER. *(Commandingly.)* Quiet! Sit down and listen. *(The children obey, sitting on the floor around the mother, who begins):*

Blood is an immense sea
that bathes all the beaches...
Men go across the blood,

navegando en sus barcazas:
reman, que reman, que reman,
¡nunca de remar descansan!
Al negro de negra piel
la sangre el cuerpo le baña;
la misma sangre, corriendo,
hierve bajo carne blanca.
¿Quién vio la carne amarilla,
cuando las venas estallan,
sangrar sino con la roja
sangre con que todos sangran?
¡Ay del que separa niños,
porque a los hombres separa!
El sol sale cada día,
va tocando en cada casa,
da un golpe con su bastón,
y suelta una carcajada...
¡Que salga la vida al sol,
de donde tantos la guardan,
y veréis como la vida
corre de sol empapada!
La vida vida saltando,
la vida suelta y sin vallas,
vida de la carne negra,
vida de la carne blanca,
y de la carne amarilla,
con sus sangres desplegadas...

(*Los niños, fascinados, se van levantando, y rodean a la madre, que los abraza formando un grupo con ellos, pegados a su alrededor. Continúa*):

Sobre sangre van los hombres
navegando en sus barcazas:
reman, que reman, que reman,
¡nunca de remar descansan!
¡Ay de quien no tenga sangre,

sailing in their barges:
they row, and row, and row,
never stop rowing!
Blood bathes the body,
of a black with black skin;
the same blood, that runs,
boils under white skin.
Yellow flesh,
when veins burst
bleeds with the same red blood
that all veins bleed.
Beware, who divides children,
also divides men!
The sun rises every day,
goes knocking at every door,
gives a blow with its stick,
lets out a burst of laughter...
Let life come out to the sun,
where so many wait for it,
and you will see that life
runs overflowing with sun!
Life, life leaping,
free life and without fences,
life for the black flesh,
life for the white flesh,
life for the yellow flesh,
with their spilled blood...

*(The children, fascinated, slowly get up and gather round the
mother, who embraces them, pulling them into a tight group.
She goes on):*

Men go across the blood
sailing in their barges:
they row, and row, and row,
they never stop rowing!
Wretched the man who has no blood,

porque de remar acaba,
y si acaba de remar,
da con su cuerpo en la playa,
un cuerpo seco y vacío,
un cuerpo roto y sin alma,
un cuerpo roto y sin alma!...

for he cannot go on rowing,
and if he stops rowing,
his body will rot on the beach,
a dry husk of a body,
a soulless broken body
a soulless broken body!...

ELEGÍAS

(1948-1958)

ELEGÍA A EMMETT TILL

El cuerpo mutilado de Emmett Till, 14 años, de Chicago, Illinois,
fue extraído del río Tallahatchie, cerca de Greenwood, el 31 de agosto,
tres días después de haber sido raptado de la casa de su tío,
por un grupo de blancos armados de fusiles...

The Crisis, New York, octubre de 1955.

En Norteamérica,
la Rosa de los Vientos
tiene el pétalo sur rojo de sangre.

El Mississippi pasa
¡oh viejo río hermano de los negros!,
con las venas abiertas en el agua,
el Mississippi cuando pasa.
Suspira su ancho pecho
y en su guitarra bárbara,
el Mississippi cuando pasa
llora con duras lágrimas.

El Mississippi pasa
y mira el Mississippi cuando pasa
árboles silenciosos
de donde cuelgan gritos ya maduros,
el Mississippi cuando pasa,
y mira el Mississippi cuando pasa
cruces de fuego amenazante,
el Mississippi cuando pasa,
y hombres de miedo y alarido
el Mississippi cuando pasa,
y la nocturna hoguera
a cuya luz caníbal
danzan los hombres blancos,
y la nocturna hoguera
con un eterno negro ardiendo,

ELEGY FOR EMMETT TILL[14]

The mutilated body of Emmett Till, fourteen years old,
from Chicago, Illinois, was recovered from the Tallahatchie River
on August 31 near Greenwood, three days after being kidnapped
from his uncle's home by a group of white men armed with rifles...

The Crisis, New York, October 1955.

In North America,
the Rose of the Winds
has a southern petal spattered with blood.

The Mississippi flows
oh, ancient river, brother of the Blacks!
its veins open in the water,
the Mississippi flows by.
Its broad chest heaves
with its wild guitar,
the Mississippi flows
full of bitter tears.

The Mississippi flows
and as the Mississippi wanders on
it sees mute trees
ripe-laden with crying moans.
The Mississippi flows by,
and as the Mississippi wanders on
it sees crosses of menacing fire,
the Mississippi flows by,
men of fear and screaming,
the Mississippi flows by,
bonfires at night,
in whose cannibal light,
white men dance;
bonfires at night
with the eternal black man burning,

un negro sujetándose
envuelto en humo el vientre desprendido,
los intestinos húmedos,
el perseguido sexo,
allá en el Sur alcohólico,
allá en el Sur de afrenta y látigo,
el Mississippi cuando pasa.

Ahora ¡oh Mississippi,
oh viejo río hermano de los negros!,
ahora un niño frágil,
pequeña flor de tus riberas,
no raíz todavía de tus árboles,
no tronco de tus bosques
no piedra de tu lecho,
no caimán de tus aguas:
un niño apenas,
un niño muerto, asesinado y solo,
negro.

Un niño con su trompo,
con sus amigos, con su barrio,
con su camisa de domingo,
con su billete para el cine,
con su pupitre y su pizarra,
con su pomo de tinta,
con su guante de béisbol,
con su programa de boxeo,
con su retrato de Lincoln,
con su bandera norteamericana,
negro.

Un niño negro asesinado y solo,
que una rosa de amor
arrojó al paso de una niña blanca.

a Black holding in
his smoke-filled spilled guts,
his moist bowels,
his tortured sex,
down in the alcoholic South,
down in the South of insult and lash,
where the Mississippi flows by.

And now, oh Mississippi,
oh ancient river, brother of the Blacks!,
now a delicate child,
a tiny flower of your banks,
still no root of your trees,
or tree-trunk in your forests,
no stone in your bed,
or a cayman[15] in your waters:
barely a child,
a dead child, murdered, alone,
black.

A boy with his top,
his friends, his neighbourhood,
his Sunday shirt,
his cinema ticket,
his desk and his blackboard,
his bottle of ink,
his baseball glove,
his boxing programme,
his Lincoln picture,
his U.S. flag,
black.

A black boy, murdered, alone,
who tossed a rose of love
at a white girl's passing by.

¡Oh viejo Mississippi,
oh rey, oh río de profundo manto!,
detén aquí tu procesión de espumas,
tu azul carroza de tracción oceánica:
mira este cuerpo leve,
ángel adolescente que llevaba
no bien cerradas todavía
las cicatrices en los hombros
donde tuvo las alas;
mira este rostro de perfil ausente,
deshecho a piedra y piedra,
a plomo y piedra,
a insulto y piedra;
mira este abierto pecho,
la sangre antigua ya de duro coágulo.
Ven y en la noche iluminada
por una luna de catástrofe,
la lenta noche de los negros
con sus fosforescencias subterráneas,
ven y en la noche iluminada,
dime tú, Mississippi,
si podrás contemplar con ojos de agua ciega
y brazos de titán indiferente,
este luto, este crimen,
este mínimo muerto sin venganza,
este cadáver colosal y puro:
ven y en la noche iluminada,
tú, cargado de puños y de pájaros,
de sueños y metales,
ven y en la noche iluminada,
oh viejo río hermano de los negros,
ven y en la noche iluminada,
ven y en la noche iluminada,
dime tú, Mississippi...

Oh ancient Mississippi,
oh king, oh deep-cloaked river!,
hold your foamy flowing parade here,
your blue ocean-bound coach:
see this light body,
this adolescent angel
bearing unhealed scars
on his shoulders
where once were wings:
a face with an absent profile,
disfigured by stone after stone,
by lead and stone,
insult and stone;
look at this open chest,
old hardened blood.
Come, and in the night made bright
by a moon of ill-omen,
the slow night of the Blacks,
with its subterranean phosphorescence,
come, and in the night made bright,
you tell me, Mississippi,
if you can watch with eyes of blinded water,
armed as an indifferent Titan,
this mourning, this crime,
this small death unavenged,
this vast and pure corpse:
come, and in the blazing night,
you – freighted with fists and birds,
dreams and metals –
come, and in the blazing night,
oh ancient river, brother of the Blacks,
come, in the blazing night,
come, in the blazing night,
tell me, Mississippi...

LA PALOMA DE VUELO POPULAR

(1958)

LA MURALLA

Para hacer esta muralla,
tráiganme todas las manos:
los negros, sus manos negras,
los blancos, sus blancas manos.
Ay,
una muralla que vaya
desde la playa hasta el monte,
desde el monte hasta la playa, bien,
allá sobre el horizonte.

— ¡Tun, tun!
— ¿Quién es?
— Una rosa y un clavel...
— ¡Abre la muralla!
— ¡Tun, tun!
— ¿Quién es?
— El sable del coronel...
— ¡Cierra la muralla!
— ¡Tun, tun!
— ¿Quién es?
— La paloma y el laurel...
— ¡Abre la muralla!
— ¡Tun, tun!
— ¿Quién es?
— El alacrán y el ciempiés...
— ¡Cierra la muralla!

Al corazón del amigo,
abre la muralla;
al veneno y al puñal,
cierra la muralla;
al mirto y la yerbabuena,
abre la muralla;
al diente de la serpiente,
cierra la muralla;

THE WALL

To build this wall
give me all your hands:
the Blacks, black hands,
the Whites, white hands.
Alas,
a wall that may stretch
from the beach to the mountain,
from the mountain to the beach, yes,
way back beyond the horizon.

"Knock-knock!"
"Who's there?"
"A rose and a carnation..."
"Open the wall!"
"Knock-knock!"
"Who's there?"
"The colonel's sword..."
"Close the wall!"
"Knock-knock!"
"Who's there?"
"The dove and the laurel..."
"Open the wall!"
"Knock-knock!"
"Who's there?"
"The scorpion and the centipede..."
"Close the wall!"

To the friend's heart,
open the wall;
to the poison and the dagger,
close the wall;
to the myrtle and the mint,
open the wall;
to the serpent's tooth,
close the wall;

al ruiseñor en la flor,
abre la muralla...

Alcemos una muralla
juntando todas las manos;
los negros, sus manos negras,
los blancos, sus blancas manos.
Una muralla que vaya
desde la playa hasta el monte,
desde el monte hasta la playa, bien,
allá sobre el horizonte...

to the nightingale on the flower,
open the wall...

Let's raise a wall
joining all our hands;
black and white hands,
white and black hands.
A wall that may stretch
from the beach to the mountain,
from the mountain to the beach, yes,
way back beyond the horizon...

CANCIÓN PUERTORRIQUEÑA

¿Cómo estás, Puerto Rico,
tú de socio asociado en sociedad?
Al pie de cocoteros y guitarras,
bajo la luna y junto al mar,
¡qué suave honor andar del brazo,
brazo con brazo del Tío Sam!
¿En qué lengua me entiendes,
en qué lengua por fin te podré hablar,
si en yes,
si en sí,
si en bien,
si en well,
si en mal,
si en bad, si en very bad?

Juran los que te matan
que eres feliz...¿Será verdad?
Arde tu frente pálida,
la anemia en tu mirada logra un brillo fatal;
masticas una jerigonza
medio española, medio slang;
de un empujón te hundieron en Corea,
sin que supieras por quién ibas a pelear,
si en yes,
si en sí,
si en bien,
si en well,
si en mal,
si en bad, si en very bad!

Ay, yo bien conozco a tu enemigo,
el mismo que tenemos por acá,
socio en la sangre y el azúcar,
socio asociado en sociedad:
United States and Puerto Rico,

PUERTO RICAN SONG

How are you, Puerto Rico,
you, member of Society's Members' Club?
At the foot of coco-palms and guitars,
beneath the moon, by the sea,
what a sweet honour to walk,
arm in arm with Uncle Sam!
In what language[16] do you understand me?
In what language, after all, should I address you,
whether in yes,
in sí,
in bien,
in well,
in mal,
in bad, in very bad?

Those killing you swear
that you are happy... Can this be true?
Your pale brow burns,
your anaemic gaze takes on a fatal brightness,
you mumble some jargon
half Spanish, half slang;
with one shove they plunged you into Korea,
without knowing for whom you were going to fight,
whether in yes,
in sí,
in bien,
in well,
in mal,
in bad, in very bad!

Oh, how well I know your enemy,
for we have the same one right here,
a member of our blood and our sugar,
a member of Society's Members' Club:
United States and Puerto Rico,

es decir New York City with San Juan,
Manhattan y Borinquen, soga y cuello,
apenas nada más...
No yes,
no sí,
no bien,
no well,
sí mal,
sí bad, sí very bad!

that is to say, New York City with San Juan,
Manhattan and Borinquen[17], noose and neck,
hardly anything else...
Not yes,
not sí,
not bien,
not well,
but mal,
yes bad, very bad!

RÍOS

Tengo del Rin, del Ródano, del Ebro,
tengo los ojos llenos;
tengo del Tíber y del Támesis,
tengo del Volga, del Danubio,
tengo los ojos llenos.

Pero yo sé que el Plata,
pero yo sé que el Amazonas baña;
yo sé que el Misisipi,
pero yo sé que el Magdalena baña;
yo sé que el Almendares,
pero yo sé que el San Lorenzo baña;
yo sé que el Orinoco,
pero yo sé que bañan
tierras de amargo limo donde mi voz florece
y lentos bosques presos en sangrientas raíces.
¡Bebo en tu copa, América,
en tu copa de estaño,
anchos ríos de lágrimas!

Dejad, dejadme,
dejadme ahora junto al agua.

RIVERS

With the Rhine, the Rhône and the Ebro,
my eyes are filled;
with the Tiber, the Thames,
the Volga, and the Danube,
my eyes are filled.

But I know that the Plata,
and I know that the Amazon laps;
but I know that the Mississippi,
and I know that the Magdalena laps;
I know that the Almendares,
but I know that the San Lorenzo laps;
and I know that the Orinoco,
I know they bathe
lands of bitter mud where my voice blooms
and languid woods imprisoned in bloody roots.
America, I drink from your cup,
from your tin cup,
great rivers of tears!

Leave me, leave me,
leave me now close to the water.

PEQUEÑA LETANÍA GROTESCA EN LA MUERTE DEL SENADOR McCARTHY

He aquí al senador McCarthy,
muerto en su cama de muerte,
flanqueado por cuatro monos;
he aquí al senador McMono,
muerto en su cama de Carthy,
flanqueado por cuatro buitres;
he aquí al senador McBuitre,
muerto en su cama de mono,
flanqueado por cuatro yeguas;
he aquí al senador McYegua,
muerto en su cama de buitre,
flanqueado por cuatro ranas:
                    McCarthy Carthy.

He aquí al senador McDogo,
muerto en su cama de aullidos,
flanqueado por cuatro gángsters;
he aquí al senador McGángster,
muerto en su cama de dogo,
flanqueado por cuatro gritos;
he aquí al senador McGrito,
muerto en su cama de gángster,
flanqueado por cuatro plomos;
he aquí al senador McPlomo,
muerto en su cama de gritos,
flanqueado por cuatro esputos:
                    McCarthy Carthy.

He aquí al senador McBomba,
muerto en su cama de injurias,
flanqueado por cuatro cerdos;
he aquí al senador McCerdo,

SHORT GROTESQUE LITANY ON THE DEATH
OF SENATOR McCARTHY

Here lies Senator McCarthy,
dead on his deathbed,
flanked by four monkeys;
here lies Senator McMonkey,
dead on his Carthy-bed,
flanked by four vultures;
here lies Senator McVulture,
dead on his monkey-bed,
flanked by four mares;
here lies Senator McMare,
dead on his vulture-bed,
flanked by four frogs:
                McCarthy Carthy.

Here lies Senator McBulldog,
dead on his howling-bed,
flanked by four gangsters;
here lies Senator McGangster,
dead on his bulldog-bed,
flanked by four screams;
here lies Senator McScream,
dead on his gangster-bed,
flanked by four bullets;
here lies Senator McBullet,
dead on his bed of screams,
flanked by four spittles:
                McCarthy Carthy.

Here lies Senator McBomb,
dead on his bed of insults,
flanked by four pigs;
here lies Senator McPig,

muerto en su cama de bombas,
flanqueado por cuatro lenguas;
he aquí al senador McLengua,
muerto en su cama de cerdo,
flanqueado por cuatro víboras;
he aquí al senador McVíbora,
muerto en su cama de lenguas,
flanqueado por cuatro búhos:
                    McCarthy Carthy.

He aquí al senador McCarthy,
                    McCarthy muerto,
                    muerto McCarthy,
                    bien muerto y muerto,
                    amén.

dead on his bed of bombs,
flanked by four tongues;
here lies Senator McTongue,
dead on his pig's bed,
flanked by four vipers;
here lies Senator McViper,
dead on his tongue's bed,
flanked by four owls:
                    McCarthy Carthy.

Here lies Senator McCarthy,
                    dead McCarthy,
                    McCarthy dead,
                    stone-cold dead, dead,
                    amen.

BARES

Amo los bares y tabernas
junto al mar,
donde la gente charla y bebe
sólo por beber y charlar.
Donde Juan Nadie llega y pide
su trago elemental,
y están Juan Bronco y Juan Navaja
y Juan Narices y hasta Juan
Simple, el sólo, el simplemente
Juan.

Allí la blanca ola
bate de la amistad;
una amistad de pueblo, sin retórica,
una ola de ¡hola! y ¿cómo estás?
Allí huele a pescado,
a mangle, a ron, a sal
y a camisa sudada puesta a secar al sol.

Búscame, hermano, y me hallarás
(en La Habana, en Oporto,
en Jacmel, en Shanghai)
con la sencilla gente
que sólo por beber y charlar
puebla los bares y tabernas
junto al mar.

BARS

I do love the bars and taverns
by the sea,
where people chat and drink
just for the sake of it.
Where John Nobody enters and asks
for his simple drink,
and meets John Raspy, John Blade
John Nostrils and even John
Simple, plain and simply
John.

There the white wave
foams with friendship;
a peoples' friendship, unadorned,
a wave of "Hi!" and "How are things?"
There it smells of fish,
mangrove, rum, salt,
and a sweaty shirt drying out in the sun.

Look for me, brother, and you will find me
(in Havana, in Oporto,
in Jacmel[18], in Shanghai)
with the simple people
who just for the sake of drinking and chatting
fill the bars and taverns
by the sea.

LA CANCIÓN DEL REGRESO

¿Conoces tú
la tierra del arroz y del bambú?
¿No la conoces tú?

Yo vengo de Pekín.
Pekín
sin mandarín,
ni palanquín.
Yo vengo de Shanghai:
no hay
ni un yanqui ya en Shanghai.

Allá
la vida en flor está.
Se ve
la vida puesta en pie.

¡Canta conmigo, amigo,
y di como yo digo!
No hay ni un yanqui ya en Shanghai.
Pekín
enterró al mandarín.
¡Corre a ver tú
la tierra del arroz y del bambú!

SONG OF RETURN

Do you know
the land of rice and bamboo?
Don't you know it?

Now, I've come from Peking.
Peking
without mandarins,
or palanquins.
Also, I have been to Shanghai:
there is
not even one Yankee in Shanghai.

Over there
life is blossoming.
You can see
how life is blooming.

Sing with me, friend
and say as I say!
Not even one Yankee in Shanghai.
Peking
buried the mandarins.
Run and see,
the land of rice and bamboo!

CIUDADES

KINGSTON

Bajo el hambriento sol
(God save the King)
negra de bata blanca
cantando una canción.
(God save the King)
Una canción.
¿Por siempre?
¿Por siempre esa canción?
Oh yes!
Oh no!
Oh yes!

Oh no!

NEW YORK

¿Y la tarde, entreabierta
como una niña pura?
¿Y el corazón decidme?
¿Habéis visto una lágrima?

CITIES

KINGSTON

Beneath the hungry sun
(God save the King)
a black woman in a white dressing gown
singing a song.
(God save the King)
A song.
Forever?
That song forever?
Oh yes!
Oh no!
Oh yes!

Oh no!

NEW YORK

And the evening, half open
like an innocent girl?
And the heart...tell me?
Have you seen a tear?

PANAMÁ

— How are you, Panamá?
— I'm well.
(El cabaret de Jimmy, el bar de Joe.)
— ¿Sí?
— Yes.

— Hermano panameño:
¿No sueñas con Hostos y Martí?
— Sueño.
— Yes?
— Sí.

MADRID

Bajo el azufre polvoriento,
un miliciano muerto,
un joven muerto, ya viejo,
se saca un árbol del pecho.
— ¿Has entendido?
                    — Entiendo

PANAMÁ

"How are you, Panamá?"
"I'm fine."
(Jimmy's cabaret, Joe's Bar)
"¿Sí?"
"Yes."

"Panamanian brother."
"Do you dream of Hostos[19] and Martí[20]?"
"I dream."
"You do?"
"I do."

MADRID

Beneath the dusty sulphur,
a dead militia-man,
a dead youth, now old,
pulls a tree from his chest.
"Did you understand?"
                              — "I did."

TENGO

(1964)

TENGO

Cuando me veo y toco
yo, Juan sin Nada no más ayer,
y hoy Juan con Todo,
y hoy con todo,
vuelvo los ojos, miro,
me veo y toco
y me pregunto cómo ha podido ser.

Tengo, vamos a ver,
tengo el gusto de andar por mi país,
dueño de cuanto hay en él,
mirando bien de cerca lo que antes
no tuve ni podía tener.
Zafra puedo decir,
monte puedo decir,
ciudad puedo decir,
ejército decir,
ya míos para siempre y tuyos, nuestros,
y un ancho resplandor
de rayo, estrella, flor.

Tengo, vamos a ver,
tengo el gusto de ir
yo, campesino, obrero, gente simple,
tengo el gusto de ir
(es un ejemplo)
a un banco y hablar con el administrador,
no en inglés,
no en señor,
sino decirle compañero como se dice en español.

Tengo, vamos a ver,
que siendo un negro
nadie me puede detener
a la puerta de un dancing o de un bar.

I HAVE

When I see and touch myself
I, John, a Nobody only yesterday,
and today John with everything,
and today with everything.
I glance around, I look,
I see and touch myself
and I wonder how could it happen.

I have, let's see,
I have the pleasure of walking through my country,
master of all there is in it,
looking very closely at that which
I couldn't have, nor could have had before.
I can say, sugarcane crop,
I can say, mountain,
I can say, city,
I can say, army,
now mine forever, yours, ours,
and a vast splendour
of sunbeam, star, flower.

I have, let's see,
I have the pleasure of going,
I, a peasant, a worker, a simple man,
I have the pleasure of going
(just an example)
to a bank and talking to the manager,
not in English,
not as 'Sir',
but calling him 'compañero' as we say in Spanish.

I have, let's see,
that being Black
no one can stop me
at the door of a dance hall or a bar.

O bien en la carpeta de un hotel
gritarme que no hay pieza,
una mínima pieza y no una pieza colosal,
una pequeña pieza donde yo pueda descansar.

Tengo, vamos a ver,
que no hay guardia rural
que me agarre y me encierre en un cuartel,
ni me arranque y me arroje de mi tierra
al medio del camino real.
Tengo que como tengo la tierra tengo el mar,
no country,
no jaláif,
no tenis y no yacht,
sino de playa en playa y ola en ola,
gigante azul abierto democrático:
en fin, el mar.

Tengo, vamos a ver,
que ya aprendí a leer,
a contar,
tengo que ya aprendí a escribir
y a pensar
y a reír.
Tengo que ya tengo
donde trabajar
y ganar
lo que me tengo que comer.
Tengo, vamos a ver,
tengo lo que tenía que tener.

Or even at the hotel reception
yelling at me there are no rooms
not a tiny room, not a large one
or a small room where I might rest.

I have, let's see,
there are no rural police
to seize me and lock me in jail
or uproot me from my land
and throw me in the middle of the highway.
Having the land, I have the sea,
no country-club,
no high life,
no tennis and no yacht
but from beach to beach and wave on wave,
gigantic, blue, open, democratic:
in short, the sea.

I have, let's see,
I've already learnt to read
to count,
I've already learnt to write,
to think,
to laugh.
I have, now,
a place to work
and I can earn
what I have to eat.
I have, let's see,
I have, what was coming to me.

¿PUEDES?

¿Puedes venderme el aire que pasa entre tus dedos
y te golpea la cara y te despeina?
¿Tal vez podrías venderme cinco pesos de viento,
o más, quizás venderme una tormenta?
¿Acaso el aire fino
me venderías, el aire
(no todo) que recorre
en tu jardín corolas y corolas,
en tu jardín para los pájaros,
diez pesos de aire fino?

      El aire gira y pasa
      en una mariposa.
      Nadie lo tiene, nadie.

¿Puedes venderme cielo,
el cielo azul a veces,
o gris también a veces,
una parcela de tu cielo,
el que compraste, piensas tú, con los árboles
de tu huerto, como quien compra
      el techo con la casa?
¿Puedes venderme un dólar
de cielo, dos kilómetros
de cielo, un trozo, el que tú puedas,
de tu cielo?

      El cielo está en las nubes.
      Altas las nubes pasan.
      Nadie las tiene, nadie.

¿Puedes venderme lluvia, el agua
que te ha dado tus lágrimas y te moja la lengua?
¿Puedes venderme un dólar de agua
de manantial, una nube preñada,

CAN YOU?

Can you sell me the air that passes through your fingers
and strokes your face and disarranges your hair?
Perhaps, you could sell me five pesos worth of wind,
or better, maybe sell me a storm?
Perhaps, you could sell me
the pure air, the air
(not all of it) which stirs
flower after flower in your garden,
in your garden for the birds,
ten pesos worth of pure air?

       The air whirls and skims
       in a butterfly.
       No one owns it, no one.

Can you sell me a bit of sky,
the sky, blue at times,
grey at others,
a bit of your sky,
the sky you think you bought
with trees from your orchard, like one who buys
       the roof with his house?
Can you sell me a dollar's worth
of sky, two kilometres
of sky, a fragment
whatever you can?

       The sky is in the clouds.
       The clouds float high.
       No one owns them, no one.

Can you sell me some rain, the water
that gave you your tears and wets your tongue?
Can you sell me a dollar's worth of water
from a spring, a full blown cloud,

crespa y suave como una cordera,
o bien agua llovida en la montaña,
o el agua de los charcos
abandonados a los perros,
o una legua de mar, tal vez un lago,
cien dólares de lago?

      El agua cae, rueda.
      El agua rueda, pasa.
      Nadie la tiene, nadie.

¿Puedes venderme tierra, la profunda
noche de las raíces; dientes
de dinosaurios y la cal
dispersa de lejanos esqueletos?
¿Puedes venderme selvas ya sepultadas, aves muertas,
peces de piedra, azufre
de los volcanes, mil millones de años
en espiral subiendo? ¿Puedes
venderme tierra, puedes
venderme tierra, puedes?

      La tierra tuya es mía.
      Todos los pies la pisan.
      Nadie la tiene, nadie.

curly and fluffy as a ewe?
Maybe mountain rain-water,
or the water in puddles
left behind for the dogs,
or a league of sea, a lake perhaps,
a hundred dollars' worth of lake?

> Water falls and runs.
> Water runs and passes.
> No one owns it, no one.

Can you sell me the earth, the deep night
of the roots; teeth
of dinosaurs, and the scattered lime
of ancient skeletons?
Can you sell me jungles, buried in time, extinct birds,
fossilized fish, the sulphur
of the volcanoes, a thousand million years
of rising spirals? Can you
sell me the earth, can you
sell me the earth, can you?

> Your earth is my earth.
> All feet walk over it.
> No one owns it, no one.

VINE EN UN BARCO NEGRERO...

Vine en un barco negrero.
Me trajeron.
Caña y látigo el ingenio.
Sol de hierro.
Sudor como caramelo.
Pie en el cepo.
Aponte me habló sonriendo.
Dije: — Quiero.
¡Oh muerte! Después silencio.
Sombra luego.
¡Qué largo sueño violento!
Duro sueño.

       La Yagruma
       de nieve y esmeralda
       bajo la luna.

O'Donnell. Su puño seco.
Cuero y cuero.
Los alguaciles y el miedo.
Cuero y cuero.
De sangre y tinta mi cuerpo.
Cuero y cuero.

Pasó a caballo Maceo.
Yo en su séquito.
Largo el aullido del viento.
Alto el trueno.
Un fulgor de macheteros.
Yo con ellos.

       La Yagruma
       de nieve y esmeralda
       bajo la luna.

I CAME ON A SLAVE SHIP...

I came on a slave ship.
They brought me.
Sugarcane and whip the plantation.
Branding sun.
Sweat like molasses.
Feet in the stocks.
Aponte[21] spoke to me, smiling.
I said: "I am willing!"
Oh death!" Afterwards, silence.
Then darkness.
Such a long forced sleep!
A harsh sleep.

> The Yagruma[22]
> emerald and snow
> beneath the moon.

O'Donnell[23]. His dry fist.
Whip and more whip.
The constables and fear.
Whip and more whip.
Blood and stains on my body.
Whip and more whip.

Maceo[24] passed on horseback.
I, in his retinue.
Long the wind's howl.
Loud the thunder.
A radiance of cane-cutters.
I, with them.

> The Yagruma
> emerald and snow
> beneath the moon.

Tendido a Menéndez veo.
Fijo, tenso.
Borbota el pulmón abierto.
Quema el pecho.
Sus ojos ven, están viendo.
Vive el muerto.

¡Oh Cuba! Mi voz entrego.
En ti creo.
Mía la tierra que beso.
Mío el cielo.

Libre estoy, vine de lejos.
Soy un negro.

      La Yagruma
      de nieve y esmeralda
      bajo la luna.

I see Menéndez[25] stretched out.
Motionless, taut.
His open lung spurting forth.
His chest burning.
His eyes are watchful, alive.
The dead man goes on living.

Oh Cuba! I surrender my voice.
I believe in you.
Mine is the land I kiss.
Mine is the sky.

I am free, I came from afar.
I am a black man.

> The Yagruma
> emerald and snow
> beneath the moon.

ESTÁ BIEN

Está muy bien que cantes cuando lloras, negro hermano,
negro del Sur crucificado:
bien tus spirituals,
tus estandartes,
tus marchas y los alegatos
de tus abogados.
Está muy bien.

Bien que patines en pos de la justicia,
— ¡oh aquel ingenuo patinador
tragando aire hasta Washington desde Chicago! —;
bien tus protestas en los diarios,
bien tus puños cerrados
y Lincoln en su retrato.
Está muy bien.

Bien tus sermones en los templos dinamitados,
bien tu insistencia heroica
en estar junto a los blancos,
porque la ley — ¿la ley? — proclama
la igualdad de todos los americanos.
                    Bien.
                    Está muy bien.
                    Requetebién,
hermano negro del Sur crucificado.
Pero acuérdate de John Brown,
que no era negro y te defendió con un fusil en las manos.

Fusil: arma de fuego portátil
(es lo que dice el diccionario)
con que disparan los soldados.
Hay que agregar: *Fusil* (en inglés <<*gun*>>):
arma también con que responden
los esclavos.

IT'S ALL RIGHT

It's all right that you sing as you cry, black brother, [it's good?]
black man from the crucified South:
your spirituals are right,
your banners,
your marches and the allegations
of your legal counsel.
It's all right.

Right that you skate in pursuit of justice,
– oh, that naive skater
swallowing air from Chicago to Washington! – ;
your protests in the dailies are right,
your clenched fists are right
and Lincoln in his portrait.
It's all right.

Your sermons in your dynamited temples are right,
right, your heroic persistence
of being together with the White,
for the law – the law? – proclaims
the equality of all Americans.
                    Right.
                    Quite right.
                    Extremely right,
black brother of the crucified South.
Don't forget John Brown, who was not a black man
and defended you armed with a rifle.

Rifle: a portable firearm
(that's what the dictionary says)
used by soldiers for shooting.
We must add: *Rifle* (in English "a long barrel gun")
a weapon also used by slaves to
answer back.

Pero si ocurre (eso acontece),
pero si ocurre, hermano,
que no tienes fusil, pues entonces,
en ese caso,
digo, no sé,
búscate algo
– una mandarria, un palo,
una piedra – algo
que duela,
algo duro que hiera,
que golpee,
que saque sangre,
algo.

But if it happens (it does sometimes),
but if it happens, brother,
that you have no rifle, well then,
in that case,
I say, I don't know,
find yourself something –
a sledgehammer, a stick,
a stone – something
that will hurt,
something hard that will wound,
that will strike,
that will shed blood,
something.

GOBERNADOR

Cuando hayas enseñado tu perro
a abalanzarse sobre un negro
y arrancarle el hígado de un bocado,
cuando también tú sepas
por lo menos ladrar y menear el rabo,
alégrate, ya puedes
¡oh blanco!
ser gobernador de tu Estado.

ESCOLARES

Cumplieron sus tareas (prácticas) los escolarizados
muchachos blancos de Alabama:
cada uno presentó una rama
de flamboyán, con cinco negros ahorcados.

GOVERNOR

When you have trained your dog[26]
to rush at a Black
and to tear his liver out with a bite,
when you can also,
bark at least and wag your tail,
rejoice, for now you can
be governor of your State,
white man!

PUPILS

The white boys from Alabama
finished their (practical) homework in school:
each of them brought in a colourful branch
decorated with five hanged Blacks.

RESPONDE TÚ...

Tú, que partiste de Cuba
responde tú,
¿dónde hallarás verde y verde,
azul y azul,
palma y palma bajo el cielo?
Responde tú.

Tú, que tu lengua olvidaste,
responde tú,
y en lengua extraña masticas
el güel y el yu,
¿cómo vivir puedes mudo?
Responde tú.

Tú, que dejaste la tierra,
responde tú,
donde tu padre reposa
bajo una cruz,
¿dónde dejarás tus huesos?
Responde tú.

Ah desdichado, responde,
responde tú,
¿dónde hallarás verde y verde,
azul y azul,
palma y palma bajo el cielo?
Responde tú.

SONES, SONNETS, BALLADS AND SONGS

ANSWER ME...

You, who left Cuba
answer me,
Where will you find so many greens,
so many blues,
and so many palm trees under the sky?
Answer me.

You, who have forgotten your language,
answer me,
and chew on a foreign language
the "well" and the "you",
how can you live silent?
Answer me.

You who left your land behind,
answer me,
where your father lies buried
under a cross,
where will you rest your bones?
Answer me.

Oh, poor wretch, answer,
answer me.
Where will you find so many greens,
so many blues,
and so many palm trees under the sky?
Answer me.

BALADA

Ay, venga, paloma, venga
y cuénteme usted su pena.

— Pasar he visto a dos hombres
armados y con banderas;
el uno en caballo moro,
el otro en potranca negra.
Dejaran casa y mujer,
partieran a lueñes tierras;
el odio los acompaña,
la muerte en las manos llevan.
¿A dónde vais?, preguntéles,
y ambos a dos respondieran:
Vamos andando, paloma,
andando para la guerra.
Así dicen, y después
con ocho pezuñas vuelan,
vestidos de polvo y sol,
armados y con banderas,
el uno en caballo moro,
el otro en potranca negra.

Ay, venga, paloma, venga
y cuénteme usted su pena.

— Pasar he visto a dos viudas
como jamás antes viera,
pues que de una misma lágrima
estatuas parecen hechas.
¿A dónde vais, mis señoras?,
pregunté a las dos al verlas.
Vamos por nuestros maridos,
paloma, me respondieran.
De su partida y llegada
tenemos amargas nuevas;

BALLAD

Come Dove, come
and tell me where it hurts.

I saw two men go by
armed and with flags;
one riding a dark horse
the other a black filly.
They left homes and wives,
set off for distant lands;
with hate as their escort,
and death in their hands.
I asked them "Where are you going?"
and they answered as one:
"We are going, Dove,
we are going to war."
So they said and then
on eight hooves they flew
dressed in dust and sun,
armed and with flags,
one riding a dark horse
the other a black filly.

Come Dove, come
and tell me where it hurts.

I saw two widows go by
that I never saw before,
they were like two statues
shaped from a single tear.
"Where are you going, my ladies?"
I asked them both.
"We are looking for our husbands,
oh Dove," they replied.
"We have bitter tidings
of their leaving and arrival;

tendidos están y muertos,
muertos los dos en la hierba,
gusanos ya sobre el vientre
y buitres en la cabeza,
sin fuego las armas mudas
y sin aire las banderas;
se espantó el caballo moro,
huyó la potranca negra.

Ay, venga, paloma, venga
y cuénteme usted su pena.

they are laid out and dead,
both dead on the grass,
worms in their stomachs,
vultures at their heads,
with silent empty guns
and flags with no wind;
the dark horse was driven away,
the black filly fled.

Come Dove, come
and tell me where it hurts.

EL GRAN ZOO

(1967)

AVISO

Por un decreto del Ayuntamiento
fue creado este Gran Zoo
para nativos y extranjeros
y orgullo de nuestra nación.
Entre los ejemplares de más mérito
están los animales de agua y viento
(como en el caso del ciclón)
también un aconcagua verdadero,
una guitarra adolescente,
nubes vivas,
un mono catedrático y otro cotiledón.

Patria o muerte!

El Director

ANNOUNCEMENT

By a resolution of the Town Council
this Great Zoo was created
for foreigners, natives
and the pride of our nation.
Among the most valuable specimens
are the animals of water and wind
(as in the case of the cyclone),
also a genuine Aconcagua,
an adolescent guitar
living clouds,
an academic monkey and a cotyledon.

Fatherland or death!

The Director

LOS RÍOS

He aquí la jaula de las culebras.
Enroscados en sí mismos,
duermen los ríos, los sagrados ríos.
El Mississippi con sus negros,
El Amazonas con sus indios.
Son como los zunchos poderosos
de unos camiones gigantescos.

Riendo, los niños les arrojan
verdes islotes vivos,
selvas pintadas de papagayos,
canoas tripuladas
y otros ríos.

Los grandes ríos se despiertan,
se desenroscan lentamente,
engullen todo, se hinchan, a poco más revientan,
y vuelven a quedar dormidos.

RIVERS

Here we have the cage of the snakes.
Coiling up on themselves
the rivers, the sacred rivers, sleep.
The Mississippi with its Blacks,
the Amazon with its Indians
They are like the powerful iron straps
of some gigantic trucks.

The children, laughing, throw
living, green islets
jungles decorated with parrots,
manned canoes
and other rivers into them.

The great rivers wake up,
slowly unwind, gulping down everything,
become swollen to the point of bursting
and fall asleep once more.

EL TIGRE

Anda preso en su jaula
de duras rayas negras.
El metal con que ruge
quema, está al rojo blanco.

(Un gánster.
El instinto sexual.
Un boxeador
Un furioso de celos.
Un general.
El puñal del amor.)

Tranquilizarse.
Un tigre
real.

THE TIGER

Imprisoned, he paces his cage
of hard black stripes.
The metal sound of his roar
burns white hot.

(A gangster.
The sexual instinct.
A boxer.
A raving, jealous lover.
A general.
Love's dagger.)

Calm down.
A real
tiger.

CICLÓN

Ciclón de raza,
recién llegado a Cuba de las islas Bahamas.
Se crió en Bermudas,
pero tiene parientes en Barbados.
Estuvo en Puerto Rico.
Arrancó de raíz el palo mayor de Jamaica.
Iba a violar a Guadalupe.
Logró violar a Martinica.
Edad: dos días.

CYCLONE

A thoroughbred cyclone
has just arrived in Cuba from the Bahamas.
It grew in Bermuda,
but has relatives in Barbados.
It visited Puerto Rico.
Uprooted the mainmast of Jamaica.
It was on its way to rape Guadeloupe.
It succeeded in raping Martinique.
Age: two days.

LYNCH

Lynch de Alabama.
Rabo en forma de látigo
y pezuñas terciarias.
Suele manifestarse
con una gran cruz en llamas.
Se alimenta de negros, sogas,
fuego, sangre, clavos,
alquitrán.
                        Capturado
junto a una horca. Macho.
Castrado.

LYNCH

Lynch of Alabama
Tail in the shape of a whip
and fraternity hooves.
Usually, it reveals itself
with a great cross ablaze.
Feeds on Blacks, ropes,
fire, blood, nails,
tar.
                Apprehended
at a hanging. Male.
Castrated.

K K K

Este cuadrúpedo procede
de Joplin, Misurí.
Carnicero.
Aúlla largamente en la noche
sin su dieta habitual de negro asado.

Acabará por sucumbir.
Un problema (insoluble) alimentarlo.

K K K

This four-footed creature comes
from Joplin, Missouri.
Flesh-eating.
It howls all night long
without its usual diet of barbecued Black.

In the end, it will perish.
Feeding it, an (insoluble) problem.

LA RUEDA DENTADA

(1972)

¿QUÉ COLOR?

«Su piel era negra, pero con el alma
purísima como la nieve blanca....»
YEVTUCHENKO (según el cable), ante
el asesinato de Lutero King

Qué alma tan blanca, dicen,
la de aquel noble pastor.
Su piel tan negra, dicen,
su piel tan negra de color,
era por dentro nieve,
azucena,
leche fresca,
algodón.
Qué candor.
No había ni una mancha
en su blanquísimo interior.

(En fin, valiente hallazgo:
«El negro que tenía el alma blanca»,
aquel novelón.)

Pero podría decirse de otro modo:
Qué alma tan poderosa negra
la del dulcísimo pastor.
Qué alta pasión negra
ardía en su ancho corazón.
Qué pensamientos puros negros
su grávido cerebro alimentó.
Qué negro amor,
tan repartido
sin color.
¿Por qué no,
por qué no iba a tener el alma negra
aquel heroico pastor?
Negra como el carbón.

WHAT COLOUR?

«His skin was black, but with the purest
soul as white as snow...»
YEVTUCHENKO (in a cable),
on the assassination of Luther King.

Such a white soul, they say,
that noble pastor had.
His skin so black, they say,
his skin so black in colour,
was on the inside snow,
a white lily,
fresh milk,
cotton-wool.
Such purity!
There wasn't one single stain
on his immaculate white interior.

(In short, what an extraordinary find:
'The Black whose soul was white',
a melodramatic tale.)

But there is another way to say it:
What an excellent black soul
the gentlest of pastors had.
What a high black passion
burned in his open heart.
What pure black thoughts
fed in his fertile mind.
What black love
widely shared
without colour.
And why not,
why couldn't that heroic pastor have
a black soul?
Black as coal.

BURGUESES

No me dan pena los burgueses
vencidos. Y cuando pienso que van a darme pena,
aprieto bien los dientes y cierro bien los ojos.
Pienso en mis largos días sin zapatos ni rosas.
Pienso en mis largos días sin sombrero ni nubes.
Pienso en mis largos días sin camisa ni sueños.
Pienso en mis largos días con mi piel prohibida.
Pienso en mis largos días.

— No pase, por favor. Esto es un club.
— La nómina está llena.
— No hay pieza en el hotel.
— El señor ha salido.
— Se busca una muchacha.
— Fraude en las elecciones.
— Gran baile para ciegos.
— Cayó el Premio Mayor en Santa Clara.
— Tómbola para huérfanos.
— El caballero está en Paris.
— La señora marquesa no recibe.

En fin, que todo lo recuerdo.
Y como todo lo recuerdo,
¿qué carajo me pide usted que haga?
Pero además, pregúnteles.
Estoy seguro
de que también recuerdan ellos.

THE BOURGEOISIE

I don't grieve over the defeated bourgeoisie.
And when I think I might,
I clench my teeth and shut my eyes tight.
I think of my long days without shoes or roses.
I think of my long days without a hat or clouds.
I think of my long days without a shirt or dreams.
I think of my long days with my forbidden skin.
I think of my long days.

"You can't come in. This is a private club."
"Sorry, no vacancies."
"No rooms free in this hotel."
"The boss is out."
"Maid required."
"Electoral fraud."
"Grand ball in aid of the blind."
"The first prize went to Santa Clara."
"Orphans charity raffle."
"The gentleman is in Paris."
"Her ladyship is not at home."

In short, I remember it all.
And as I remember it all,
what the hell would you expect me to do?
What's more, ask them.
I'm sure
they also remember it too.

DIGO QUE YO NO SOY UN HOMBRE PURO

Yo no voy a decirte que soy un hombre puro.
Entre otras cosas
falta saber si es que lo puro existe.
O si es, pongamos, necesario.
O posible.
O si sabe bien.
¿Acaso has tú probado el agua químicamente pura,
el agua de laboratorio,
sin un grano de tierra o de estiércol,
sin el pequeño excremento de un pájaro,
el agua hecha no más que de oxígeno e hidrógeno?
¡Puah! qué porquería.

Yo no te digo pues que soy un hombre puro,
yo no te digo eso, sino todo lo contrario.
Que amo (a las mujeres, naturalmente,
pues mi amor puede decir su nombre),
y me gusta comer carne de puerco con papas,
y garbanzos y chorizos, y
huevos, pollos, carneros, pavos,
pescados y mariscos,
y bebo ron y cerveza y aguardiente y vino,
y fornico (incluso con el estómago lleno).
Soy impuro ¿qué quieres que te diga?
Completamente impuro.
Sin embargo,
creo que hay muchas cosas puras en el mundo
que no son más que pura mierda.
Por ejemplo, la pureza del virgo nonagenario.
La pureza de los novios que se masturban
en vez de acostarse juntos en una posada.
La pureza de los colegios de internado, donde
abre sus flores de semen provisional

I STATE THAT I AM NOT A PURE MAN

I will not tell you I am a pure man.
Among other things,
we don't know if anything pure exists.
Or it is, let's say, necessary.
Or it is possible.
Or if it has a good flavour.
Have you ever drank chemically pure water,
laboratory water,
without a grain of dirt or manure,
without a bird's small droppings,
water formed only by oxygen and hydrogen?
Yuck! What muck!

Well, I am not going to tell you I am a pure man;
I will not tell you that, but the complete opposite.
That I love (women, naturally,
for my love can speak its name).
I like to eat pork with potatoes,
chickpeas, pork sausages,
eggs, chicken, mutton, turkey,
fish and seafood.
I drink rum, beer, hard liquor, wine,
and fornicate (sometimes on a full stomach).
I am an impure man, what do you want me to tell you?
Totally impure.
Nevertheless,
I think there are many pure things in the world
that are nothing but pure shit.
For example, the purity of a ninety-year-old hymen.
The purity of the sweethearts who masturbate
instead of going to bed together in some hotel.
The purity of boarding schools
where a fauna of pederasts

la fauna pederasta.
La pureza de los clérogos.
La pureza de los académicos.
La pureza de los que aseguran
que hay que ser puros, puros, puros.
La pureza de los que nunca tuveron blenorragia.
La pureza de la mujer que nunca lamió un glande.
La pureza del que nunca succionó un clitoris.
La pureza de la que nunca parió.
La pureza del que no engendró nunca.
La pureza del que se da golpes en el pecho, y
dice santo, santo, santo,
cuando es un diablo, diablo, diablo.
En fin, la pureza
de quien no llegó a ser lo suficientemente impuro
para saber qué cosa es la pureza.

Punto, fecha y firma.
Así lo dejo escrito.

opens its blooms of provisional semen.
The purity of the clergy.
The purity of the academics.
The purity of the grammarians.
The purity of those who assure us
that we must be pure, forever pure.
The purity of those who have never suffered from pox.
The purity of the woman who has never licked a prick.
The purity of the man who has never sucked a clitoris.
The purity of the woman who has never given birth.
The purity of the man who has never planted a seed.
The purity of the one who beating his breast
says holy, holy, holy;
when he is a devil, devil, devil.
In brief, the purity
of whoever was never sufficiently impure
for knowing what purity is.

Full stop, date and signature.
Thus, I leave it in writing.

CHE COMANDANTE

No porque hayas caído
tu luz es menos alta.
Un caballo de fuego
sostiene tu escultura guerrillera
entre el viento y las nubes de la Sierra.
No por callado eres silencio.
Y no porque te quemen,
porque te disimulen bajo tierra,
porque te escondan
en cementerios, bosques, páramos,
van a impedir que te encontremos,
Che Comandante,
amigo.

Con sus dientes de júbilo
Norteamérica ríe. Mas de pronto
revuélvese en su lecho
de dólares. Se le cuaja
la risa en una máscara,
y tu gran cuerpo de metal
sube, se disemina
en las guerrillas como tábanos,
y tu ancho nombre herido por soldados
ilumina la noche americana
como un estrella súbita, caída
en medio de una orgía.
Tú lo sabías, Guevara,
pero no lo dijiste por modestia,
por no hablar de ti mismo,
Che Comandante,
amigo.

Estás en todas partes. En el indio
hecho de sueño y cobre. Y en el negro

CHE COMANDANTE[27]

Your light shines no less high
just because you fell.
A horse of fire
raises your warrior's shape
from between the winds and clouds of the Sierra.
Not because they stopped your mouth are you silent.
Though they burn you,
hide you underground,
concealed in cemeteries,
forests and high barren plateaus,
they won't prevent us finding you.
Che Comandante,
my friend.

North America laughs
with jubilant teeth. Soon to turn
over and over in its bed
of dollars. Its laugh
freezing into a mask
and your great steel body
rising to spread among
the guerrillas like gadflies,
and your broad name, wounded by soldiers
lights up the American night
like a sudden star, falling
into the midst of an orgy.
You knew it, Guevara,
but modestly didn't say it,
not wishing to boast.
Che Comandante,
my friend.

You are everywhere. In the Indian
forged of drowsiness and copper. In the Black

169

revuelto en espumosa muchedumbre,
y en el ser petrolero y salitrero,
y en el terrible desamparo
de la banana, y en la gran pampa de las pieles,
y en el azúcar y en la sal y en los cafetos,
tú, móvil estatua de tu sangre como te derribaron,
vivo, como no te querían,
Che Comandante,
amigo.

Cuba te sabe de memoria. Rostro
de barbas que clarean. Y marfil
y aceituna en la piel de santo joven.
Firme la voz que ordena sin mandar,
que manda compañera, ordena amiga,
tierna y dura de jefe camarada.
Te vemos cada día ministro,
cada día soldado, cada día
gente llana y difícil
cada día.
Y puro como un niño
o como un hombre puro,
Che Comandante,
amigo.

Pasas en tu descolorido, roto, agujereado traje de campaña.
El de la selva, como antes
fue el de la Sierra. Semidesnudo
el poderoso pecho de fusil y palabra,
de ardiente vendaval y lenta rosa.
No hay descanso.

                        ¡Salud, Guevara!
O mejor todavía desde el hondón americano:
Espéranos. Partiremos contigo. Queremos
morir para vivir como tú has muerto,

stirring in crowds of foam;
in the oil worker, in the saltpetre worker
and in the terrible wastes
of bananas, in the great pampa of hides,
in sugar, in salt, and in coffee bushes,
you, a moving statue of blood as they shoot you through,
alive, like they did not want you.
Che Comandante,
my friend.

Cuba knows you by heart. A face
with a shiny beard. The skin of
a young saint, olive and ivory.
A firm voice that commands without tyranny,
leading as a companion, giving orders like a friend,
warm and firm as a chief and a comrade.
We see you daily a minister,
each day a soldier, each day
a simple and obstinate person
each day.
Pure as a child
or as a man pure.
Che Comandante,
my friend.

Passing in your faded, torn and ragged fighting clothes.
The clothes you wore in the jungle,
as you did before in the Sierra. Half-naked
full-chested, mighty with rifle and words,
of burning winds and gentle rose.
There is no rest.

                Long live, Guevara!
Or better still, from the American depths:
Wait for us. We will leave together. We want
to die to live, as you have died,

para vivir como tú vives,
Che Comandante,
amigo.

to live as you live,
Che Comandante,
my friend.

GUITARRA EN DUELO MAYOR

I

Soldadito de Bolivia,
soldadito boliviano,
armado vas de tu rifle,
que es un rifle americano,
que es un rifle americano,
soldadito de Bolivia,
que es un rifle americano.

II

Te lo dio el señor Barrientos,
soldadito boliviano,
regalo de míster Johnson
para matar a tu hermano,
para matar a tu hermano,
soldadito de Bolivia,
para matar a tu hermano.

III

¿No sabes quién es el muerto,
soldadito boliviano?
El muerto es el Che Guevara,
y era argentino y cubano,
y era argentino y cubano,
soldadito de Bolivia,
y era argentino y cubano.

GUITAR IN D(EATH) MAJOR

I

Soldier boy from Bolivia,
Bolivian soldier,
carrying your rifle,
your American rifle,
your American rifle,
soldier boy from Bolivia,
your American rifle.

II

Señor Barrientos[28] gave it to you,
Bolivian soldier,
a present from Mister Johnson
to kill your brother with,
to kill your brother with,
soldier boy from Bolivia,
to kill your brother with.

III

Do you know who the dead man is,
Bolivian soldier?
The dead man is Che Guevara,
he was Argentinian and Cuban,
he was Argentinian and Cuban
soldier boy from Bolivia
he was Argentinian and Cuban.

IV

Él fue tu mejor amigo,
soldadito boliviano;
él fue tu amigo de a pobre
del Oriente al altiplano,
del Oriente al altiplano,
soldadito de Bolivia,
del Oriente al altiplano.

V

Está mi guitarra entera,
soldadito boliviano,
de luto, pero no llora,
aunque llorar es humano,
aunque llorar es humano,
soldadito de Bolivia,
aunque llorar es humano.

VI

No llora porque la hora,
soldadito boliviano,
no es de lágrima y pañuelo,
sino de machete en mano,
sino de machete en mano,
soldadito de Bolivia,
sino de machete en mano.

IV

He was your best friend,
Bolivian soldier;
he was your friend in poverty
from Oriente to the high plateau,
from Oriente to the high plateau,
soldier boy from Bolivia,
from Oriente to the high plateau.

V

My guitar is in full mourning,
Bolivian soldier,
but it does not cry,
though crying is human,
though crying is human,
soldier boy from Bolivia,
though crying is human.

VI

This is no time to cry,
Bolivian soldier,
no time for drying our tears,
it is a time to wield the machete,
it is a time to wield the machete,
soldier boy from Bolivia,
it is a time to wield the machete.

VII

Con el cobre que te paga,
soldadito boliviano,
que te vendes, que te compra,
es lo que piensa el tirano,
es lo que piensa el tirano,
soldadito de Bolivia,
es lo que piensa el tirano.

VIII

Despierta, que ya es de día,
soldadito boliviano,
está en pie ya todo el mundo,
porque el sol salió temprano,
porque el sol salió temprano,
soldadito de Bolivia,
porque el sol salió temprano.

IX

Coge el camino derecho,
soldadito boliviano;
no es siempre camino fácil,
no es fácil siempre ni llano,
no es fácil siempre ni llano,
soldadito de Bolivia,
no es fácil siempre ni llano.

VII

With the coppers he pays you,
Bolivian soldier,
that you sell yourself, he buys you,
thus the tyrant's mind turns,
thus the tyrant's mind turns,
soldier boy from Bolivia,
thus the tyrant's mind turns.

VIII

Wake up, it's daybreak already,
Bolivian soldier;
everybody is already up,
for the sun rose early,
for the sun rose early,
soldier boy from Bolivia,
for the sun rose early.

IX

Take the straight road,
Bolivian soldier;
it's not always the easy road,
not always smooth or easy,
not always smooth or easy,
soldier boy from Bolivia,
not always smooth or easy.

X

Pero aprenderás seguro,
soldadito boliviano,
que a un hermano no se mata,
que no se mata a un hermano,
que no se mata a un hermano,
soldadito de Bolivia,
que no se mata a un hermano.

X

But you are bound to learn,
Bolivian soldier,
that you must not kill your brother,
that you must not kill your brother,
that you must not kill your brother,
soldier boy from Bolivia,
that you must not kill your brother.

EL DIARIO QUE A DIARIO

(1972)

AVISOS, MENSAJES, PREGONES

Prologuillo no estrictamente necesario

Primero fui el notario
polvoriento y sin prisa,
que inventó el inventario.
Hoy hago de otra guisa:
soy el diario que a diario
te previene, te avisa
numeroso y gregario.
¿Vendes una sonrisa?
¿Compras un dromedario?
Mi gran stock es vario.
Doquier mi planta pisa
brota lo extraordinario.

PROBLEMAS DE PURISMO. Stock, voz inglesa.
Doquier, arcaismo. Mas para nuestra empresa, todo es uno y
lo mismo.

LA DIRECCIÓN

WARNINGS, MESSAGES, PUBLIC PROCLAMATIONS

Short prologue, not strictly required

Firstly, I was the notary,
covered with dust and unrushed,
creator of the inventory.
Today, I have a different role:
I am the Daily that every day
forewarns and puts you on your guard,
in a rhythmical and gregarious way.
Are you selling a smile?
Or do you wish to buy a dromedary?
My large stock is varied.
Wherever my foot treads down
the extraordinary is found.

PROBLEMS OF PURISM. Stock, Anglicism.
Wherever, archaism. But for our management, all is one and
the same.

THE MANAGEMENT

ESCLAVOS EUROPEOS

ADVERTENCIA IMPORTANTE

Es sorprendente la semejanza que existe
entre el texto de estos anuncios y el lenguaje
empleado por los traficantes en esclavos
africanos (negreros) para proponer
su mercancía. Forzados por la costumbre
general aceptamos su publicación, no sin
consignar la repugnancia que tan infame
comercio produce en nuestro espíritu.

Sobre la venta y compra de esclavos, jóvenes y en perfecta
salud, y también acerca de fugas de los mismos, su cambio
por objetos de interés vario, así en la vida pública como
familiar:

EUROPEAN SLAVES

IMPORTANT NOTICE

> The resemblance between the text of these
> notices and the language used by the African
> slave traders (slave-drivers) to advertise their
> merchandise, is extraordinary.
> Compelled by common practice, we agreed
> to print them, but not without stating the
> disgust that such vile commerce brings to
> our soul.

Concerning the purchase and sale of slaves, young and in perfect
health, and also with regard to the escape of such slaves, their
exchange for various types of objects, in public and domestic life:

VENTAS

Véndese un blanco joven, calesero
de una o de dos bestias;
general cocinero
y más que regular repostero.
Impondrán
en casa de D. Pedro Sebastián,
al 15½ de Teniente Rey
donde además se arrienda un buey.

Dos blancas jóvenes por su
ajuste: en la calle de Cuba
casa No. 4 impondrán.

Blanca de cuatro meses de parida, sin rasguño ni
una herida, de buena y abundante leche, regular lavandera,
criolla cocinera, sana y sin tacha, fresquísima
muchacha: EN 350 PESOS LIBRES PARA EL
VENDEDOR, EN LA CALLE DE LA PALOMA,
AL No. 133.

Una pareja de blanquitos, hermanos de 8 y 10 años
macho y hembra, propios para distraer niños de su
edad. También una blanquita (virgen) de 16. En la
calle del Cuervo, al 430, darán razón y precio.

SALES

Young, white male for sale, Calash driver
can drive one or two beasts:
general cook
and more than average confectioner.
For more information
contact Don Pedro Sebastián
at 15½ of Teniente Rey,
where an ox is also for hire.

Two young white females
for hire: More information
at house No.4, Cuba Street.

White girl, gave birth four months ago, without
scratch or injury, plentiful and good quality milk,
average laundress, Creole cook, healthy and undamaged,
extremely youthful: GO TO No. 133
DOVE STREET, WITH 350 PESOS, TAX-FREE,
FOR THE VENDOR.

A pair of white children, brother and sister, ages 8 and 10,
suitable for entertaining children of their own ages. Also
for sale, a young 16 year old blond girl (a virgin).
Price and more information at No. 430 Crow Street.

CAMBIO

Se cambia un blanco libre de tacha
por una volanta de la marca Ford
y un perro.
Casa Mortuoria de la Negra Tomasa,
junto at Callejón del Tambor.
(segunda cuadra después de la plaza)
darán razón.

FUGA

Ha fugado de casa de su amo
un blanco de mediana estatura,
ojos azules y pelo colorado,
sin zapatos,
camisa de listado
sobre fondo morado.
Quien lo entregue
será gratificado.
San Miguel, 31,
estramuros,
casa que llaman del Tejado.

EXCHANGE

Flawless white male
to be exchanged for a Ford
two-wheeled carriage and a dog.
Funeral Parlour of Black Tomasa,
next to Drum Lane
(second block after the square)
for more information.

ESCAPE

A medium height, white male
has escaped from his master's house;
he has blue eyes, red hair,
bare feet.
He was wearing
a royal purple striped shirt.
Whoever hands him over
will be rewarded.
San Miguel, 31,
outside the walls,
house known as the Shed.

ACTO DE JUSTICIA

El blanco Domingo Español será conducido el viernes
próximo por las calles de la Capital llevando una navaja
colgada al cuello, misma con que causó heridas
a sus amos, un matrimonio del que era esclavo.
Le darán ciento cincuenta azotes de vergüenza
pública, y cincuenta más en la picota situada en la calle
de este nombre. Después que sane del látigo será
enviado a Ceuta por diez años.

ACT OF JUSTICE

Next Friday, the white slave Domingo Español
will be paraded through the streets of the Capital
with a flick-knife hanging from his neck;
the same flick-knife used to slash his masters,
a married couple to whom he belonged.
He will receive one hundred and fifty lashes
for his public shame: fifty more at the pillory
in the Picota Street. After the healing of his wounds,
he will be sent to Ceuta[29] for ten years.

INDEX OF FIRST LINES

INDEX OF FIRST LINES IN ENGLISH

NOTES

1. *Taita:* title of respect given to a venerable old Black man.

2. *güije:* (Cuba): This is an example of a divination poem, a sacred process by which a diviner, *santero* in Cuba, attempts to identify and sometimes eliminate the causes, real or imagined, of some tragic event. (see J.B. Kubayanda, *The Poet's Africa: Africa in the poetry of Nicolás Guillén and Aimé Césaire.*).

3. *ñeque:* Jinx, a person who brings bad luck, an evil spell.

4. *Changó*: The Yoruba god of thunder and lightning.

5. *mayombé*: A sect observing rituals devoted to a Yoruba goddess. (See Kubayanda, *The Poet's Africa*, Chapter Six, for the argument that 'one of the strengths of Caribbean poetry is the ease with which it pulls together different African experiences. English readers may recall D.H. Lawrence's poem 'The Snake' for an interesting comparison, but with a different resonance.

6. *nelumbos*: Indian lotus.

7. *multicephalous*: from the Greek, kephalè = head. From the late 18th century, Craniometry the measurement of skulls, became an integral tool of racial clasification. Here Guillén is referring to the racial mixture of Caribbean peoples.

8. *Babbitt:* Babbitt is the archetypical 'average' Midwest American businessman, a real-estate broker. The 'hero' of Sinclair Lewis's novel *Babbitt* (1922).

9. *Mauser:* German rifle widely used in colonial wars.

10. *Federico*: Federico refers to Federico García Lorca (1899-1936), the most famous and internationally best known Spanish poet who was murdered in Granada, his home town, by Francoists early in the Civil War in 1936. At present, an attempt is being made to identify his grave and body as part of a nation-wide attempt by relatives to trace the bodies of those dumped in mass graves. For the death of Lorca see Ian Gibson, *Federico García Lorca: A Life*, London, Faber and Faber, 1989.

11. *son*: Cuban popular dance music.

12. *Yoruba Lucumí:* Afrocuban "nations". Fernando Ortiz estimated that Cuban slaves were drawn from 40 different tribal groups. The Yoruba, divided into many tribes, came from what is now Western Nigeria. Slaves from the Lucumí region inland were known as Lucumis. Slaves were often simply named after the region from which they were drawn, as in the case of the Congo. Mandingos from the Mandinga group were highly prized for their intelligence and skills, and were drawn from the region between what is now Senegal and Liberia. Some acted as middlemen in the slave trade. The Carabalí came from the region drained by the Calabar region.

13. *Chinese:* As many as 125,000 Chinese were imported into Cuba as indentured labourers from the 1850s. Those who remained intermarried. Elsewhere in the Caribbean the Chinese were imported after slavery had been abolished, but not so in Cuba, where slavery was not abolished until the 1880s. There are few identifiable Chinese in Cuba today.

14. *Till:* Emmett Till was reputed to have whistled at the daughter of a local shopkeeper. He was kidnapped, beaten and shot one year before the Montgomery Black boycott of 1956. This was one of countless outrages which were commonplace in the Southern States. His mother devoted her life to trying to secure justice for her son's death. Sadly, she died too soon to

hear that the Supreme Court has just decided to reopen the case.

15. *cayman*: alligator of the genus *cayman* of tropical America.

16. *language:* the reference to language in the first stanza is interesting in view of the declaration of Spanish as the official language of Puerto Rico.

17. *Borinquen:* aboriginal and poetic name of Puerto Rico. The name means land of the noble lord.

18 *Jacmel:* a port on the south coast of Haiti.

19. *Hostos:* Eugenio María Hostos (1839-1903). A Puerto Rican patriot who campaigned for the liberation of Puerto Rico from Spanish rule. Like Martí, much of his life was spent in exile especially in his adopted home, the Dominican Republic, vowing not to return until Puerto Rico became independent.

20. *Martí:* José Martí (1853-95). The 'Apostle' is the iconic hero of Cuban independence. Poet, journalist and diplomat, he was well known throughout Spanish America in his life-time (though less so in Cuba because of Spanish censorship) through his journalism and literary works. Exiled to Spain at the age of 16 for his anti-Spanish views, the rest of his life was devoted to the cause of Cuban independence. Most of his life was spent in exile, especially in the United States, where he organized the Cuban Revolutionary Party among Spanish immigrants. One of the most perceptive critics of United States society, his insights are only now beginning to be appreciated by American critics. He died in battle in the early months of the war against Spain in 1895. He has been the inspiration for every Cuban political party and the most important influence on Fidel Castro. His essay 'Our America' should be read by anyone interested in the Americas. His complete works run to 27 volumes.

21. *Aponte:* José Antonio Aponte organised an abortive slave revolt in 1811. A free black, he recognized that with the accelerating sugar expansion neither the slave trade nor slavery would be abolished. Hence his attempt to overthrow Spanish rule by force. He was captured and executed in 1812: his head and hands were displayed as a warning.

22. *Yagruma:* trumpet creeper, plant with trumpet-shaped flowers.

23. O'Donnell: Leopoldo O'Donnell (1808-67). He was Captain General of Cuba from 1843-8. Notorious for his suppression of the *Conspiración de la Escalera*, in 1844, Cuba's largest slave revolt. One of the many killed after the revolt was the mulatto poet '*Plácido*'.

24. *Maceo:* Antonio Maceo (1848-96). Popularly known as 'The Bronze Titan' was, together with José Martí, the most popular leader of Cuban independence. The greatest of the rebel generals, he was often distrusted because of his colour but for Blacks he is their great hero from the war. He died in battle in 1896, one year after Martí.

25. *Menéndez:* Jesús Menéndez, whom Guillén knew well, was a black leader of sugarcane workers who was murdered in 1948. His death was the theme of one of Guillén's longest and greatest poems: 'Elegía a Jesús Menéndez'.

26. *dog:* the reference will not have the historical resonance for English dog-lovers that it has for Cuban Blacks who will recall the fierce mastiffs trained by slave-catchers (*ranchadores*) to hunt down maroons – escaped slaves. For a pictorial representation, see the massive painting by Richard Asdell, *The Hunted Slaves*, in the Walker Art Gallery, Liverpool.

27. *Ernesto Guevara,* nicknamed Che, was born in Argentina, son of radical parents. Trained to be a doctor, he travelled as a

student, by motorcycle, through Spanish America. This convinced him of the need for revolution if the endemic diseases (which he saw as caused by poverty) were to be eradicated. After involvement in the abortive Guatemalan Revolution (1954) he met Fidel Castro, then exiled in Mexico City, joining him in the guerrilla expedition to Oriente, in Cuba. He served as a doctor with the guerrilla army in the Sierra Maestra. After the success of the campaign against Batista, he was appointed President of the National Bank and became an emissary for the Cuban Revolution in Algeria and the Soviet Union. Irked by the life of a bureaucrat, Che left Cuba to lead other guerrilla expeditions in the Congo (1965) and in Bolivia, both of which were failures. Captured by the Bolivian army, he was executed in 1967, his bones eventually being returned to Cuba in 1997. The famous photograph, casually taken in 1960, was to become arguably the greatest iconic image of the twentieth century and is still endlessly reproduced. An excellent introduction to his life with rare photographs is *The Che Handbook* (eds. Hilda Barrio and Gareth Jenkins, MQ Publications, London, 2003.

28. *Barrientos:* General René Barrientos was the populist military president in Bolivia during the period between 1965-1967 when Che Guevara was leading his guerrilla campaign in the countryside. Barrientos, a popular figure among the peasantry, died in an air crash in 1969, two years after Che had been killed in Barrientos' campaign against him.

29. *Ceuta*: A small Spanish enclave on Morocco's Mediterranean coast. (It gained limited autonomy in 1994.) Together with Fernando Po it was used to imprison Cuban exiles.

RECOMMENDED READING

This is a selection from the large number of critical works on Guillén as well as some more general books which place him in the wider context of Caribbean literature and Cuban history.

Guillén's poetry has been collected in *Obra Poética*, vol. I, 1920-58; vol. II, 1958-72, La Habana, Instituto del Libro, 1972-3. For his prose and journalism see *Prosa de Prisa*, 3 vols. 1929-1972, La Habana, 1975-76. For a selected translation of his poetry see *Man-Making Words: Selected poems of Nicolás Guillén*, translated and annotated with an introduction by Robert Marquez and David Arthur McMurray, Amherst, University of Massachusetts Press, 1972.

The fundamental guide to Guillén's life, written by a close friend since the 1920s, is Angel Augier, *Nicolás Guillén: estudio biográfico-crítico,* La Habana, Ediciones Unión, 1984. To this should be added the important selection of criticism, with a very revealing interview with Guillén, a comprehensive bibliography and chronology, by Nancy Morejón (ed.), *Recopilación de textos sobre Nicolás Guillén,* Habana, Casa de las Américas, 1974. Her study *Nación y mestizaje en Nicolás Guillén*, La Habana Ediciones Unión, 1982, is well worth reading. Guillén was her mentor in the development of her career as a leading Cuban poet.

For historical background, two general histories can be recommended, Hugh Thomas, *Cuba: The Pursuit of Freedom*, New York, Harper & Row, 1971; new edition Da Capo, 1998; and Louis Pérez, *Cuba: Between Reform and Revolution*, Oxford, Oxford University Press, 1995. For specific aspects of Cuban history in Guillén's formative years, see Louis Pérez, *Cuba under the Platt Amendment, 1902-1934*, Pittsburgh, University of Pittsburgh Press, 1986. The war of 1898 is succinctly discussed in Louis Pérez, *The War of 1898: The United States in History and Historiography*, Chapel Hill, University of North Carolina Press, 1998. More international in scope is Angel Smith and Emma Dávila-Cox, *The Crisis of 1898: Colonial Redistribution and Nationalist Mobilization*, London, MacMillan, 1999. The best account in English of the myth and ideology of the Cuban Revolution is Antoni Kapcia, *Cuba: Island of Dreams*, Oxford, Berg Publishers, 2000. Indispensable for understanding the dynamic of modern Cuban history.

A major critical study, from a Marxist perspective, and especially useful for locating Guillén within a wider historical framework and in the context of European and Spanish American literary theories is Keith Ellis, *Cuba's Nicolás Guillén: Poetry and Ideology*, Toronto, Toronto University Press, 1983. Two books are fundamental for the analysis of the African roots of Guillén's poetry. Firstly, Ian Isidore Smart, *Nicolás Guillén: Popular Poet of the Caribbean*, Columbia, University of Missouri Press, 1990. He relates Guillén's poetry to other Caribbean writers, arguing that they all share deep African roots which he analyses in great detail. His essay, 'Discovering Nicolás Guillén through Afrocentric Literary Analysis', which castigates the 'falsehoods of white supremacist scholarship' is in Conrad James and John Perivolaris (eds.) *The Cultures of the Hispanic Caribbean*, London, MacMillan, 2000. (This book is crucial for Hispanic Caribbean writing as a whole).

Secondly, Josaphat Kubayanda, *The Poets' Africa: Africanness in the Poetry of Nicolás Guillén and Aimé Césaire*, New York, Greenwood Press, 1990. More specifically focussed on the comparison between Francophone and Afro-Hispanic poetry, he shows compellingly how 'the invented primitive becomes for these Afrocentric poets an auspicious, healing and revitalizing consciousness.' See especially page 79 for an analysis of the 'Ballad of the Güije' and pages 102-108 for the concept of jitanjáfria and Sensamayá.

Some of the wider theoretical issues raised by Black literature, although not specifically in Guillén, are discussed in Henry Louis Gates (ed.) *Black Literature and Literary Theory*, London, Methuen, 1984. For broad overviews of Black writers in the Americas and the Caribbean see O.R. Dathorne, *Dark Ancestor: the Literature of the Black Man in the Caribbean*, Baton Rouge, Louisiana State University Press, 1981, and Richard L. Jackson, *Black Writers in Latin America*, Albuquerque, University of New Mexico Press, 1979. For a succinct introduction in Spanish there is Leslie N. Wilson, *La Poesía Afroantillana*, Miami, Ediciones Universal, 1979.

For Cuban writers on Black themes, the fundamental work is William Luis, *Literary Bondage: Slavery in Cuban Narrative*, Austin, University of Texas Press, 1990. Manzano's *Autobiography of a Slave* is in a useful bilingual edition, edited and with an introduction by Ivan A. Schulman, Detroit, Wayne University Press, 1996. The rarity of slave narratives in Cuba (a dearth shared with the Anglophone

Caribbean in marked contrast to the United States) makes it worthwhile to compare Manzano with Miguel Barnet's *Autobiography of a Runaway Slave*, ed. Alistair Hennessy, London, MacMillan 1993 (2nd. edition forthcoming). Echoes of Africa in this work contrast with their absence in Manzano. Miguel Barnet's Walter Rodney Lecture, *The African Presence in Cuban Culture*, Warwick University, 1986, is a useful short introduction.

Two authors have written unusual and perceptive essays on Guillén. The first is Vera Kutzinski, 'The Carnivalization of Poetry: Nicolás Guillén's Chronicles' in her book *Against the American Grain: Myth and History in William Carlos Williams, Jay Wright and Nicolás Guillén*, Baltimore, Johns Hopkins University Press, 1987. Earlier she had translated *El Diario que a Diario*, as *The Daily Daily* with an introduction, Berkeley, University of California Press, 1979. The second is Antonio Benítez Rojo's 'Nicolás Guillén: Sugar Mill and Poetry' in his *The Repeating Island: the Caribbean and the Postmodern Perspective*, translated by James E. Maraniss, 2nd edition, Durham, Duke University Press, 1990 – an incomparable essay in an incomparable book.

The key meeting between Langston Hughes and Guillén in 1930 is covered in Arnold Rampersad's *The Life of Langston Hughes*, Oxford, Oxford University Press, 1986, vol. I, pp. 177-181. For Guillén in the Spanish Civil War see his articles in *Prosa de Prisa*, op. cit., vol. I and more generally Alistair Hennessy in the chapter on Cuba in Mark Falcoff and Frederick B. Pike (eds.) *The Spanish Civil War, 1936-39: American Hemispheric Perspectives*, Lincoln, University of Nebraska Press, 1982. An unusual (as always) short essay by G. Cabrera Infante, who knew Guillén as a colleague, 'A Poet of a Popular Parnassus' is in his *Mea Cuba*, London, Faber and Faber, 1994.

Finally, the crucial book for understanding the revolution in Cuban popular culture is that by Robin D. Moore, *Nationalizing Blackness: Afro Cubanismo and Artistic Revolution in Havana 1920-1940*, Pittsburgh, University of Pittsburgh Press, 1997, which illustrates, in particular the emergence of the *son* as the first Black street genre to gain national acceptance.

Alistair Hennessy

CHRONOLOGY

1902   Born in Camagüey.

1917   Father killed in political conflict.

1920   Enters Havana University to read law: leaves a year later.

1925   The Puerto Rican Luis Palés Matos publishes some Afro-American poetry.

1930   Meets Langston Hughes in Havana. Publishes *Motivos de son*. Imp. Rambla, Bouza y Cía., Havana. Federico García Lorca visits Havana.

1931   Publishes *Sóngoro cosongo*, *Poemas mulatos*. Ucar, García y Cía., Havana.

1933   Revolution in Cuba which lasts for 4 months.

1934   Fulgencio Batista seizes power (remains in power until 1944), and again 1952-58.

1934   Publishes *West Indies, Ltd.* Poemas, Ucar, García y Cía., Havana.

1935   The Spanish communist party poet Rafael Alberti visits Havana.

1937   Nicolás Guillén visits Mexico where he publishes *Cantos para soldados y sones para turistas*. Editorial Masas, Mexico. Travels to Spain as a delegate to the Second International Congress of Writers in the Defense of Culture. Meets Langston Hughes again and other Latin American writers. Joins the Communist party. Also publishes *España, poema en cuatro angustias y una esperanza*. Ed. México Nuevo, Mexico.

1938   Returns to Cuba and becomes editor of *Hoy*, official communist party daily.

1947   Publishes *El son entero. Suma poética, 1929-1946*. Ed. Pleamar, Buenos Aires, Argentina.

1951   Publishes *Elegía a Jesús Menéndez*. Ed. Páginas, Havana.

1952-58 During the Fulgencio Batista dictatorship goes into exile, travels widely and lives in Paris.

1954   Awarded Lenin Prize for Peace.

1958   Publishes *La paloma de vuelo popular. Elegías.* Ed. Losada, Buenos Aires, Argentina.

1959   Fulgencio Batista is overthrown by Fidel Castro on the 1st January.

1961   Proclaimed Cuba's National Poet. President of the Union of Cuban Writers and Artists (UNEAC).

1964   Publishes *Tengo*. Editorial del Consejo Nacional de Universidades, Universidad Central de las Villas, Havana.

1967   Publishes *Che Comandante*. Poema, Instituto del Libro, Havana. Also *El gran zoo*. Ed. Unión, Havana.

1972   Publishes *El diario que a diario* and *La rueda dentada*. Ed. UNEAC, Havana.

1982   Publishes *Páginas vueltas*, his first volume of memoirs.

1989   Dies in Havana.

CONTRIBUTORS

Alistair Hennessy is Emeritus Professor of History at the University of Warwick, and is at present Honorary Research Fellow at the University of Liverpool. At Warwick he founded the School of Comparative American Studies and was Director of the Centre for Caribbean Studies. He has published widely in Spanish, Latin American, Argentine, Mexican and Cuban history. He is general editor of the Macmillan's University of Warwick Caribbean Series of monographs and has edited and contributed to many volumes, including Miguel Barnet, *Esteban Montejo; the Autobiography of a Runaway Slave*. He is at present working on José Martí and José Rizal: a comparison in iconic nationalism, as well as a comparative study of empires and surrogate imperialism.

Salvador Ortiz-Carboneres was Senior Language Tutor at the Language Centre, University of Warwick. A specialist in intensive teaching, he has given intensive Spanish courses in Sweden, Poland, Italy and also wrote and taught on the BBC course "España Viva". His name frequently appeared in the *Times Educational Supplement* under reviews for Spanish teaching texts and critical appraisal. Among his published translations are poems by Nicolás Guillén and Miguel de Unamuno. His translation of *Platero and I,* by the Spanish Nobel Prize-winner Juan Ramon Jiménez, was published in 1990. Other publications include articles on the Spanish Poets, Federico García Lorca and Antonio Machado, and books such as *Journey Through Spanish Literature* and *Latin American History.* He believes that the source of true poetry is to be found in the people – *el pueblo*.